The schools' guide to the
INTERNET

Peter McBride

Heinemann Educational Publishers
Halley Court, Jordan Hill, Oxford, OX2 8EJ
a division of Reed Educational & Professional Publishing Ltd
Heinemann is a registered trademark of Reed Educational & Professional Publishing Ltd

OXFORD FLORENCE PRAGUE MADRID ATHENS
MELBOURNE AUCKLAND KUALA LUMPUR SINGAPORE TOKYO
IBADAN NAIROBI KAMPALA JOHANNESBURG GABARONE
PORTSMOUTH NH (USA) CHICAGO MEXICO CITY SAO PAULO

© Peter McBride, 1998

First published 1998

ISBN 0 435 54714 3

02 01 00 99 98
10 9 8 7 6 5 4 3 2 1

Edited by Catherine McGregor
Cover design: ie Design

Typeset by P.K.McBride, Southampton

Printed and bound by The Bath Press, Bath

Publishing team
Editorial
Philip Ellaway, Sarah Caton

Design
Phil Richards, Colette Jacquelin

Production
David Cooke

Thanks to...
Jenny Hastings and Ben Walsh of the NCET (now BECTA); to Finbar McGaughey of Research Machines; to Sam Crane, Martin Felton, Maddy Fryatt and Liz Kelsey of Regent's Park School (not forgetting the Web team – Becky, Joyce, Holly, Laura, Lindsey, Louise and Nikki); to Susan Martin, Mark Owen, Harry Dodds and the many other Web page authors whose work enlivened the hours spent on the Net researching this book.

About this book

The Internet offers superb opportunities to schools. It's the largest library in the World, the fastest postal service and the biggest showcase. It's also fast-changing, disorganised and not 100% reliable! But don't worry about it. The secret to success with the Internet is to accept that you will never fully master it. You don't need to understand all its intricacies. You don't need to know where everything is. You don't need to pick up every change as it occurs.

All you need to make good use of the Internet is a general understanding of what is possible, competence in a few basic skills, and a knowledge of where to go to search for things and how to search when you get there. This book aims to give you those things. Thus armed, you can find the material that you need, and communicate with your (old and new) friends and colleagues around the world.

If and when you want to use the Internet more actively and interactively, you can find most of the tutorials, software and samples that you need on the Internet.

This book is intended as a practical introduction for teachers and students. It assumes that there is someone in the school – or that you will bring in a local specialist – to deal with the technical matters of setting up connections, hardware and software.

- ◆ **Chapter 1** gives a general outline and introduces some of the tools and techniques that you need to get started.

- ◆ **Chapters 2 and 3** show you how to find material on the World Wide Web, either by using directories and other starting points, or by searching. And **Chapter 4** gives just a brief glance at range of sites that are now on the Web.

- ◆ **Chapter 5** covers e-mail – the simplest, fastest and cheapest way to communicate with people, near or far.

- ◆ **Chapter 6** is for the more adventurous! As well as drawing material from the Internet, you can publish your own pages for others to read. Creating a Web site is not difficult – it just takes time, a few basic skills and plenty of enthusiasm.

- ◆ In **Chapter 7** I have tried to give some ideas and point to some sites that could be useful for work in different areas of the curriculum.

- ◆ There are things to be considered before a school starts to use the Internet in earnest. **Chapter 8** aims to help you start thinking about these.

Getting to grips with the Internet is a challenge, but it's fun.

P.K.McBride

macbride@tcp.co.uk

Contents

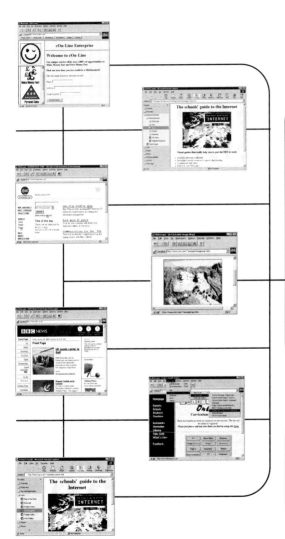

1 Internet basics

This chapter outlines the essentials of the Internet and looks at two of the most commonly-used Web browsers. Once you have got the hang of how a browser works, you are ready to go on-line!

At the end is a summary of the jargon that you are likely to meet as you travel the Internet.

Things you need to know

The Internet is not the World Wide Web

The *Internet* is a network of computers, which can communicate and share data with each other.

The *World Wide Web* is one way of looking at the resources of the Internet. It is the most important, the most useful and the most fun, but there are other ways.

E-mail is the second most important Internet activity. There are also *newsgroups*, where people can discuss common interests; *FTP*, for transferring files between distant computers; and other more specialised ways of using the Internet.

This book concentrates on the World Wide Web and e-mail.

The Internet is huge

There are over 16 million computers providing information and services for the Internet; over 1 million sites; over 10 million visitors a day to some of the most popular sites; probably almost 100 million people with access to the Internet; several hundred million documents and files can be read or viewed through the World Wide Web.

Whatever your interest, there is almost certainly something about it, somewhere on the Internet – the problem is finding it! This book will show you how.

Patience is a virtue

It takes far longer to get a page of text and images over the Internet that it does from a disk on your computer. And if the Internet is really busy at the time, it takes even longer. Be patient! It's usually worth waiting for.

There's a lot of jargon out there

You can ignore quite a lot of it, but some is essential, which is why there are a few pages on it at the end of this chapter. When you find a word **highlighted like this**, you can look it up on pages 14 to 16.

Things go wrong

When you get data from a remote computer, it reaches you through a mixture of high-speed cables, microwave links and public telephone lines, and may have passed through a dozen other computers along the way. It's not surprising that things sometimes go wrong – in fact, it's more surprising that it works as well as it does!

Windows rules

There's masses of Windows software for Internet users; a good selection for Apples and Unix computers; not much for Acorn systems. This book is geared towards Windows.

Aspects of the Internet

The World Wide Web

This is probably the most exciting and useful aspect of the Internet for most people. The Web consists of countless numbers of pages, held in over a million computers scattered across the world. They are joined together by *hypertext* links. (The address of a page is attached to some text or an image in another page, in such a way that clicking on the text or image takes you to the linked page.)

Finding the right place to start can be the trickiest bit, but once you find a page on a topic, it will often have hypertext links to others on the same topic. Net *directories* such as Yahoo (page 18) have organised sets of links to pages, and are good places to start your travels around the Web.

Most pages are illustrated with graphics, though some keep to simple, but fast, text-only displays. Some have video or sound clips; other have links to files – programs, documents or pictures – that you can download onto your computer. Some pages act as places where users can meet and chat – by typing or by talking.

To view the pages and to follow the links you need a *browser*. The two most commonly used are Netscape (see page 4) and Internet Explorer (page 6) – both of which are available for PCs and Apple Macintosh computers. Archimedes have their own browsers.

E-mail

E-mail allows you to communicate and exchange files quickly and cheaply with other Internet users. You can send a message half way round the world in minutes, and all it costs is a few seconds of telephone time. See Chapter 5.

Newsgroups

There are over 25,000 *newsgroups*, each dedicated to a specific topic. Only a few newsgroups are directly relevant to UK schools, and they are more for staff than pupils.

Newsgroups are accessed through a *news server* – a computer at your *service provider*'s site. Some service providers only carry articles from selected newsgroups.

FTP

FTP stands for File Transfer Protocol and is the standard method for copying files across the Internet. FTP hosts hold archives that are (usually) open to anyone to search and *download* files from. Some *host computers* have directories into which you can *upload* files, so that other people can share them.

You can download files through a Web browser, but to upload you normally need a dedicated FTP program.

Netscape Navigator

The Toolbar

The latest browser from Netscape is Navigator 4.0, which is part of the **Communicator** suite, but the earlier Netscape 3.0 is still widely used – and with good reason. It does the job just as well, but is smaller and faster to get started. I prefer Netscape 3.0, and it is the one that I have used for most of the screenshots in this book. If you have the even earlier Netscape 2.0, or the new Navigator, you will find a few minor differences in appearance, but all the essential functions work in the same way.

The browser window

The menu bar is always visible. Beneath this are more controls, which can be removed if they are not wanted.

◆ The **Toolbar** should be kept visible. Its buttons make browsing much simpler.

◆ The **Location** shows the current page. You can type an URL (page 10) here to go to a site. The last 10 URLs that you typed are held in its drop-down list.

◆ The **Directory** buttons link to pages on Netscape's site and can be good places to start from. These links are also on the Directory menu.

⇦o	Back to previous page
o⇨	Next page (if you have visited it, then returned to a previous page)
🏠	Home page
⟳	Reload current page
🖼	Load the images on the current page
⇨o	Open a location
🖨	Print – wait until the page is fully loaded before printing
🔍	Find text within the current page
⬤	Stop loading

If you want to change to Netscape 3.0 or upgrade to Communicator, the software can be downloaded free from Netscape's home site at:
  http://www.netscape.com

Communicator also includes:
◆ Mailbox which handles e-mail.
◆ Discussions where you can read – and write – newsgroup articles.
◆ Composer for creating Web pages. It is almost exactly the same as the old Netscape Editor (see page 102).

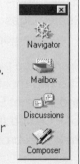

Title of current page

Address of current page

Drop-down list of URLs you have entered

Menu bar

Toolbar

Location

Directory buttons

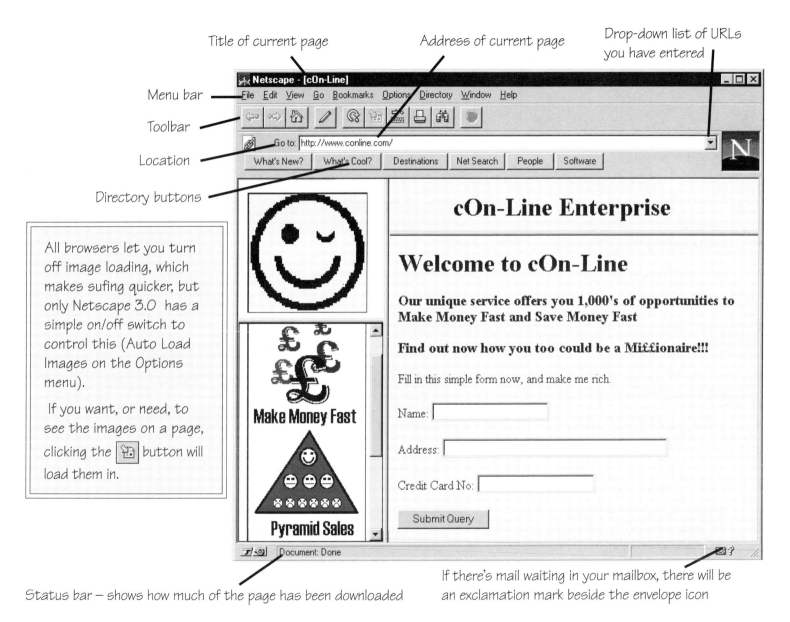

Netscape - [cOn-Line]

File　Edit　View　Go　Bookmarks　Options　Directory　Window　Help

Go to: http://www.conline.com/

What's New?　What's Cool?　Destinations　Net Search　People　Software

N

cOn-Line Enterprise

Welcome to cOn-Line

Our unique service offers you 1,000's of opportunities to Make Money Fast and Save Money Fast

Find out now how you too could be a Mi££ionaire!!!

Fill in this simple form now, and make me rich.

Name:

Address:

Credit Card No:

Submit Query

Make Money Fast

Pyramid Sales

Document: Done

All browsers let you turn off image loading, which makes sufing quicker, but only Netscape 3.0 has a simple on/off switch to control this (Auto Load Images on the Options menu).

If you want, or need, to see the images on a page, clicking the ⟨image⟩ button will load them in.

Status bar – shows how much of the page has been downloaded

If there's mail waiting in your mailbox, there will be an exclamation mark beside the envelope icon

Internet Explorer

The browser

At the time of writing, the latest Internet Explorer is 4.0. It compares well with the Netscape browsers in its speed and range of features.

Explorer gives you:

◆ An excellent screen layout. The panel on the left can be used to display the Favorites (page 13) and History lists, or for running a *search engine*. Pages selected from here are then displayed in the main window. This is particularly useful when you are flicking between sites.

◆ Safer surfing. Access can be limited to approved sites only (see page 144).

On the other hand:

◆ Internet Explorer 4.0 only works on Windows 95/98/NT or Apple Macintosh systems.

◆ Its versions of *Java* and *JavaScript* are non-standard, so the Java applets and JavaScript routines that you meet on Web pages may not run properly.

◆ It is a large program and relatively slow to get up and running.

◆ Explorer tends to take control of your system. It installs files in many places – mainly in the Windows folder – and replaces some core Windows 95 files. It also checks selected Web sites and automatically downloads new *drivers* and other updates, unless you stop it doing so. This is not a disadvantage if you are happy to let Microsoft root around in your hard drive so that it can optimise your system.

The buttons of the **Standard** toolbar are all you really need while browsing. The **Address** and **Links** toolbars can be resized or turned off if not wanted, using the **View** menu.

The left-hand panel – the **Explorer bar** – displays the Search, Favorites, History or Channels lists. It can be opened or closed as needed.

Internet Explorer 4.0 can be downloaded from Microsoft's site at

http://www.microsoft.com

but it is very large (over 60Mb with all the trimmings) and will take ages to download.

You would do better to look for it on the CDs that grace the covers of most PC magazines.

Close Explorer bar

Open list in Explorer bar

Back to previous page

Stop loading

Reload

Next page

Start page

Remove the frame

Start Mail and News

Drag to move or resize the bars

Explorer bar – great for navigating, but easily closed when you want a full screen display.

The History is a set of links to the places you have visited in the past few days.

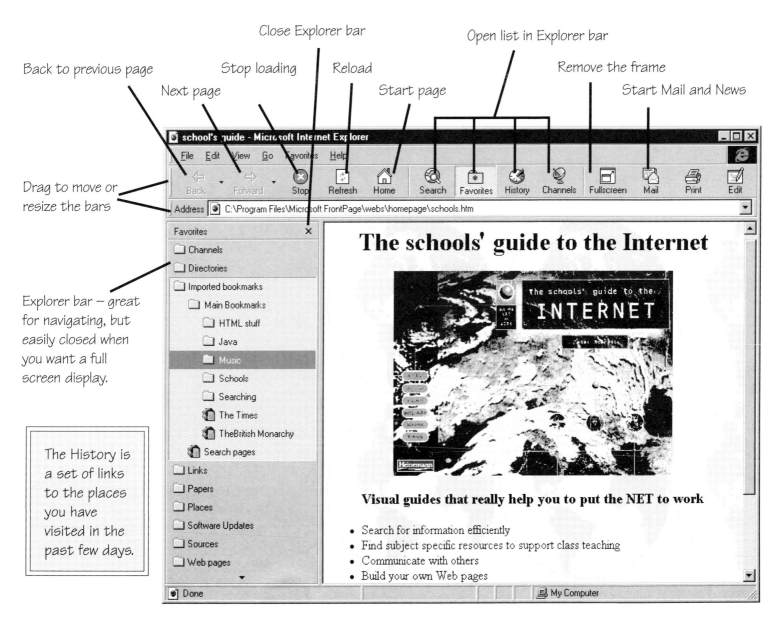

Browsers and the Web

Browsers perform two main jobs:

◆ display the pages at Web sites;

◆ **navigate** the hypertext links that take you from one page to another.

The links may be words embedded in the text, or set by themselves or presented as a list. They may also be built into pictures. Links are almost always easy to spot.

◆ Text links are underlined and normally shown in a different colour to other text.

◆ Picture links are usually outlined.

With any link, if you point at it, the cursor changes to 🖑 and the Status line shows the address of the linked page.

The linked page may be within the same site or on a far-distant one.

Some pages are dead-ends, which is when the Back button comes in handy!

Click here to return to the previous page

Click anywhere on a linked picture

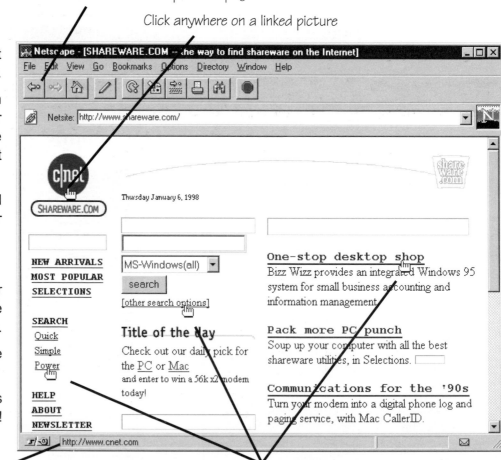

The address of the linked page is shown here

Hypertext links are usually underlined and coloured blue

Image maps

Image maps are a special type of hypertext-linked graphic. These can have any number of links embedded in them, each in its own area of the image.

In some image maps, like the Internet Resources Metamap it is clear what each part links to. In others, you have to look harder. When you see the hand icon, you are pointing to a link.

Look for the hand

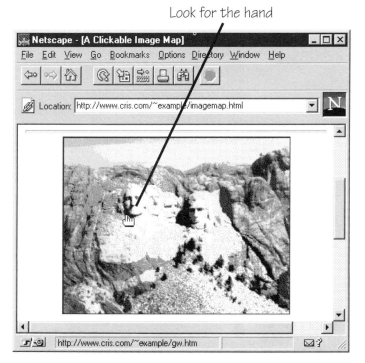

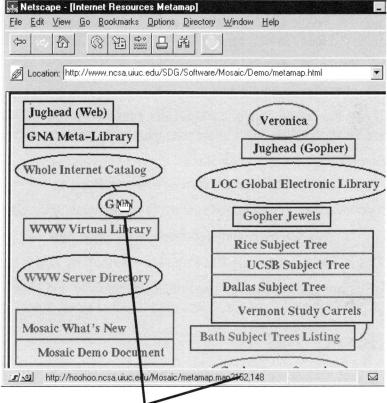

With image maps, the status bar does not show the URL when you are point to a link. All it shows is where the cursor is on the map.

9

WWW URLs

Don't you just love the TLAs (Three-Letter Acronyms)? The Internet is full of them. A **WWW URL** is a World Wide Web Uniform Resource Locator and it gives the location of a page.

The URL may be a simple name:

http://www.cnet.com

This is the home page of the c|net site. **http://** says that it is a WWW URL. **www** is how World Wide Web addresses usually (but not always) start.

Some URLs are more complex:

http://www.shareware.com/SW/Search/Popular

If you want to go to a specific page, its name must be included in the URL:

http://www.eyesoftime.com/teacher/ukpage.htm

This is The School Page UK. Page names normally end in '.htm' or '.html'.

URLs are case-sensitive – you must use capitals and lower case as they are given in the URL. You must also get the punctuation right!

Using URLs

All Web browsers have routines for entering URLs. In Netscape and Internet Explorer they can be typed into the Location (or Address) slot, or into the Open dialog box that is reached from the File menu.

The example shows how to open a URL in Netscape. You do it in much the same in all browsers. The File menu will have an Open Page or Open Location command, and if there is a Location slot, you can type the URL directly into it.

Saving text and images

If you want to save the material on a Web page, you can do one of three things.

Use the File > Save As command to save the whole page as an HTML file. Notice that this saves the text and layout only – not its images.

Highlight text and use Edit > Copy to capture it, then Paste it into a word-processor files.

Right click on an image to open the shortcut menu and select Save Image As.

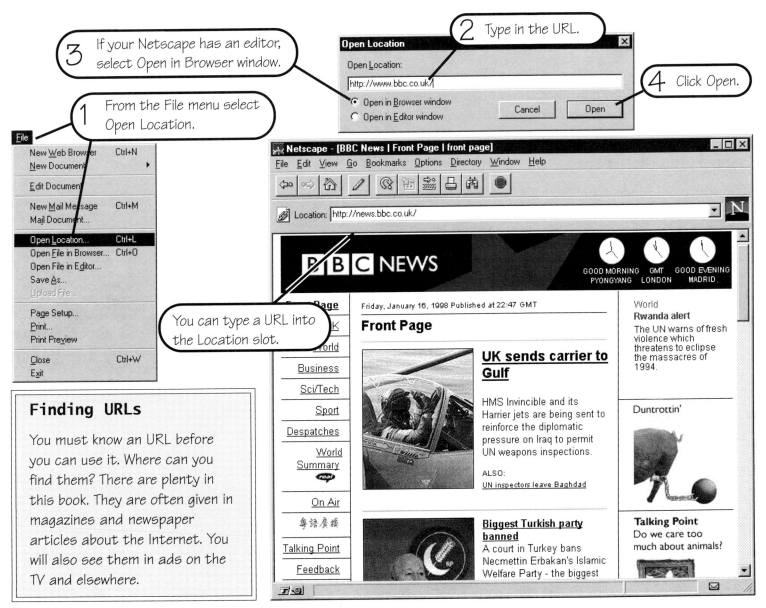

3 If your Netscape has an editor, select Open in Browser window.

2 Type in the URL.

4 Click Open.

Open Location

Open Location:

http://www.bbc.co.uk/

○ Open in Browser window
○ Open in Editor window

Cancel   Open

1 From the File menu select Open Location.

File

New Web Browser	Ctrl+N
New Document	▶
Edit Document	
New Mail Message	Ctrl+M
Mail Document...	
Open Location...	Ctrl+L
Open File in Browser...	Ctrl+O
Open File in Editor...	
Save As...	
Upload File...	
Page Setup...	
Print...	
Print Preview	
Close	Ctrl+W
Exit	

You can type a URL into the Location slot.

Netscape - [BBC News | Front Page | front page]

File Edit View Go Bookmarks Options Directory Window Help

Location: http://news.bbc.co.uk/

BBC NEWS

GOOD MORNING   GMT   GOOD EVENING
PYONGYANG   LONDON   MADRID

Friday, January 16, 1998 Published at 22:47 GMT

Front Page

Front Page
UK
World
Business
Sci/Tech
Sport
Despatches
World Summary
On Air
粵語廣播
Talking Point
Feedback

UK sends carrier to Gulf

HMS Invincible and its Harrier jets are being sent to reinforce the diplomatic pressure on Iraq to permit UN weapons inspections.

ALSO:
UN inspectors leave Baghdad

Biggest Turkish party banned
A court in Turkey bans Necmettin Erbakan's Islamic Welfare Party - the biggest

World
Rwanda alert
The UN warns of fresh violence which threatens to eclipse the massacres of 1994.

Duntrottin'

Talking Point
Do we care too much about animals?

Finding URLs

You must know an URL before you can use it. Where can you find them? There are plenty in this book. They are often given in magazines and newspaper articles about the Internet. You will also see them in ads on the TV and elsewhere.

Netscape Bookmarks

Really good places are hard to find, so when you do find one, add it to your Bookmarks. To return to it, you can then simply open the Bookmarks menu and select its title of the page.

Organising Bookmarks

When the menu starts to get crowded, organise your Bookmarks into folders. These act as sub-menus.

Use the **Go to Bookmarks...** option to open the Bookmark window. Here you can create folders and drag items into them, or delete old Bookmarks.

> 1 When you find a good page, click Add Bookmark on the Bookmarks menu.

> 3 Organise them.

> 2 To return to the page, open Bookmarks, work through the sub-menus and click on its title.

> 4 Create a folder beneath the selected item.

Explorer Favorites

Adding a Favorite

Explorer Favorites are the same as Netscape Bookmarks. The Favorites list does not start empty. Explorer adds its own Links buttons and Channels, as well as Microsoft's on-line Clip Gallery and your My Directory folder (if present) – that's right, you can surf your hard disk!

The list can be opened from the Favorites menu, or in the Explorer bar by clicking the Favorites icon in the toolbar. This can be the most convenient approach if you want to visit several Favorite places in succession.

This is done through the Favorites menu, *not*the icon. When you add one, you can edit its name (pages don't always have clear titles), or choose to store it in a folder.

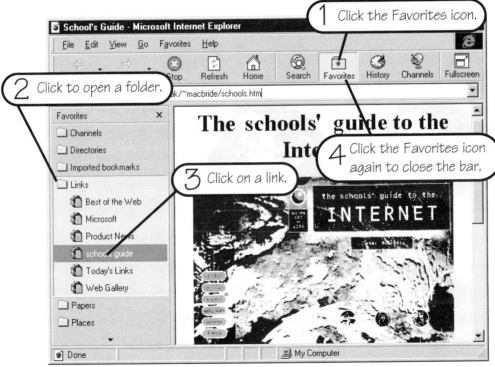

1 Click the Favorites icon.

2 Click to open a folder.

3 Click on a link.

4 Click the Favorites icon again to close the bar.

1 Open the Favorites menu and click Add to Favorites.

To create folders, move or delete items, use Organize Favorites. Folders and items are managed almost the same as in My Computer or Windows Explorer.

13

Jargon

Access provider

An organisation that links schools, businesses and home users to the Internet. Also called *service provider*.

ASCII

American Standard Code for Information Interchange. ASCII characters are the letters, digits and punctuation symbols used in ordinary text.

Bandwidth

The capacity of the communications lines – how much data can be transferred in a second. Also taken to mean on-line time, as in 'that Web site is a waste of bandwidth'.

Bookmark

The address of a Web page, saved in the browser so that you can revisit in future. Called 'Favorites' in Internet Explorer.

Browser

A program that lets you surf the *World Wide Web*. It can display Web pages, and handle the links between them.

Byte

The basic unit of computer data. A byte can hold a single character or a number between 0 and 255 (which may be part of a bigger number).

Directory

A Web site with sets of links – typically thousands! – organised by subject, to provide jumping off points into the World Wide Web.

Download

Copy a Web page or other file from a remote computer to a disk in your own machine.

Driver

Program which the computer uses to control a printer, modem, screen or other device.

E-mail (Electronic mail)

Messages sent over the Internet. E-mail is much quicker and cheaper, and about as reliable as snail mail (the good old Post Office). *See Chapter 5.*

FAQ (Frequently Asked Questions)

At lots of places on the Internet, you will find a FAQ list – a set of common questions, and their answers. Do check the FAQ first, before asking for help.

Freeware

Software for free! There are gigabytes of free programs to be found on the Internet. (See page 54.) They range from top-flight products like the Explorer and Netscape browsers, down to programs written by enthusiastic beginners.

Gigabyte

A thousand megabytes or 1,000,000,000 bytes. You could store the text of around 2,000 thick paperbacks in 1Gb!

Gopher

This was a first attempt to make the Internet more accessible. It has been overtaken by the far friendlier Web, though you will still meet some Gopher menus, mainly in university sites.

Home page

The top page of a Web site – the first one you see when you get there, unless you give the *URL* of a specific page within the site. See page 10.

Host computer

One that provides a service for Internet users. The service may be simple pages of information, access to files for downloading, a place to meet and chat with other users, or a complex interactive service.

HTML (HyperText Markup Language)

The system used to create Web pages. It is not actually a language, but a set of codes that tell a browser how to display text and images, and how to handle links between pages.

HTTP (HyperText Transport Protocol)

The agreed standard for moving hypertext files – Web pages – across the Internet, between a host computer and the browser in your machine.

Hypertext

Documents linked so that clicking on a button, icon or keyword takes you into the related document – wherever it may be. Web pages are written in *HTML*.

Java

The programming language used to create applets (small programs) that can be embedded in Web pages. Java applets can be interesting, useful and/or fun but take a while to download.

JavaScript

A simpler programming language that can be used to make Web pages more active or interactive. Often used to make text scroll in the status line at the bottom of browsers. Wow!

Login

Connect to the Internet (or any computer system). The verb does not follow the normal rules. 'Login' is one word, but it splits for other tenses – 'logged in' and 'logging in'.

Navigating

Moving around within a site, or jumping from one page to another on the World Wide Web.

Network

A collection of linked computers. On a LAN (Local Area Network), users can share printers and other resources within a building. On any network – including the Internet – users can communicate and share data with each other.

News server

A computer at an Internet access provider's site that collects newsgroup articles for the benefit of its members.

Newsgroup

A kind of electronic notice board where enthusiasts can publish and read articles about their special interest.

Search engine

A Web site which keeps an up-to-date database of pages on the Web. The best have indexed millions of pages but can give you a set of links on any topic within seconds.

Service provider

An organisation that offers a service to Internet users. Some simply offer access to the Net (access providers); some give access plus special service to their members; other provide news, reviews, file stores, on-line shopping, etc. to the public.

Shareware

Try-before-you-buy software. It can be downloaded and used for a limited time for free, but you must pay a small fee to continue to use it. Typical costs are around £15 to £30.

Upload

Copy a file from your machine onto a host computer. To publish your school's Web site, you will have to upload its pages to your access provider's server.

URL (Uniform Resource Locator)

The address of a file or page on the Internet. See page 10.

Web, WWW, W3, (World Wide Web)

Two meanings - First, loosely used: the whole constellation of resources that can be accessed using Gopher, FTP, HTTP, telnet, Usenet, WAIS and some other tools. Second, the universe of hypertext servers (HTTP servers) which are the servers that allow text, graphics, sound files, etc. to be mixed together.

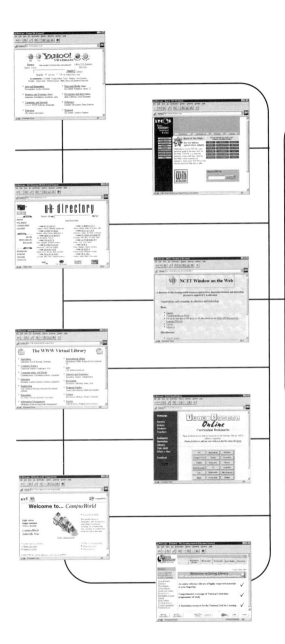

2 The World Wide Web

This chapter show you how to find your way around the Web. It shows how to get from one place to another, and how to get to a known Web page. It also introduces some places to start your travels around the Web.

You must know how to get on-line from your system and how to start up your browser.

Yahoo

Some people seem to think that Yahoo is the centre of the Web or the only way into it. It isn't – but Yahoo is one of the best places to start. It has more links than anywhere else, and is well organised.

Yahoo can be found at several places. The original Yahoo is at:

http://www.yahoo.com

Yahoo UK & Ireland is at:

http://www.yahoo.co.uk

Using Yahoo

The top level menu lists broad areas of interest with sub-categories.

◆ Click on a main heading to get a full list of its sub-categories, or

◆ If you see a sub-heading that covers the topic you want, click on it to go straight to the next level of menus.

Expect to go through at least two, and maybe four or more levels of menus to get to any real meat.

Click on a main heading to see the full list of categories in that area

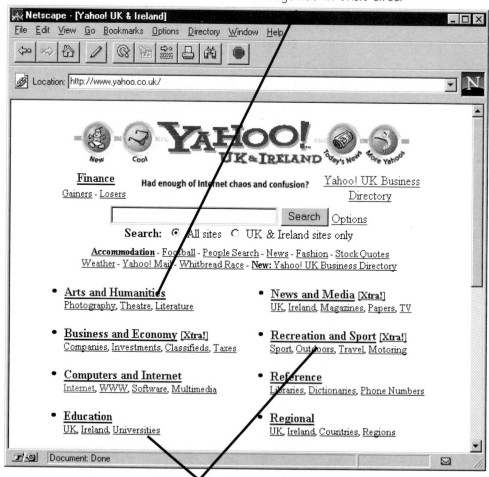

An underline shows that text is a hypertext link – click on it to jump to the linked page

Menu pages

The contents of menu pages vary, but you will always find a Search box at the top (see the next page).

At the top are links to other main menus – and to UK Only menus if you are at Yahoo UK.

The central area lists related categories and those of the next level down.

Beneath these are links to pages, with a brief description of each.

If a page (outside Yahoo) consists purely of links to relevant pages, and not information, Yahoo stores it in Indices.

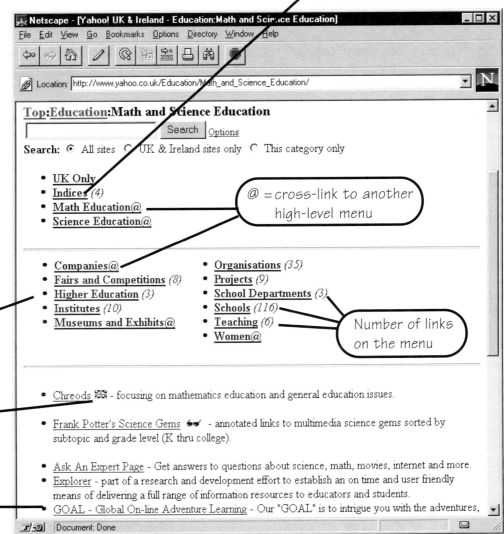

@ = cross-link to another high-level menu

The next level of menus

Number of links on the menu

At Yahoo UK, links to UK sites are listed at the top, with a Union Jack beside the name

If you could scroll down, you would see that this page had 15 links – some have 100 or more

Searching Yahoo

If you are looking for information on a specific topic, or don't know which menu to start on, try running a search.

A search will give you a list of menu categories, and a list of links that contain the given word(s).

Simple search

A simple search looks for pages that contain matches for all the words you enter.

If you limit the search you may get fewer, but more useful results.

◆ If you are in the UK, select **UK & Ireland sites only** if you are looking for companies or societies, where being local is important.

◆ If you know you are in the right menu, select **This category only**.

> The Search only finds links within Yahoo.

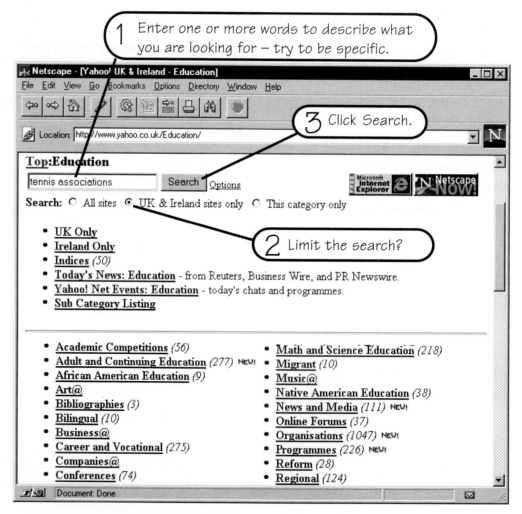

1 Enter one or more words to describe what you are looking for – try to be specific.

3 Click Search.

2 Limit the search?

Top:Education

tennis associations   Search Options

Search: ○ All sites ⦿ UK & Ireland sites only ○ This category only

- **UK Only**
- **Ireland Only**
- **Indices** *(50)*
- **Today's News: Education** - from Reuters, Business Wire, and PR Newswire.
- **Yahoo! Net Events: Education** - today's chats and programmes.
- **Sub Category Listing**

- **Academic Competitions** *(56)*
- **Adult and Continuing Education** *(277)* NEW!
- **African American Education** *(9)*
- **Art@**
- **Bibliographies** *(3)*
- **Bilingual** *(10)*
- **Business@**
- **Career and Vocational** *(275)*
- **Companies@**
- **Conferences** *(74)*
- **Math and Science Education** *(218)*
- **Migrant** *(10)*
- **Music@**
- **Native American Education** *(38)*
- **News and Media** *(111)* NEW!
- **Online Forums** *(37)*
- **Organisations** *(1047)* NEW!
- **Programmes** *(226)* NEW!
- **Reform** *(28)*
- **Regional** *(124)*

It's OK – you don't have to type this in!! This is just the search routine telling you what it's looking for.

Words within words

This Search picks up words in larger words. For example, if you entered 'lute music' it would look for pages with 'lute', 'lutes', 'flute' or 'flutes' and with 'music', 'musical' or 'musicians'.

Click to list just the Categories or the Sites, or go to AltaVista (see page 38)

4 When the results appear, go to a Category to see a menu of related links, or ...

5 ... go to a Web Site.

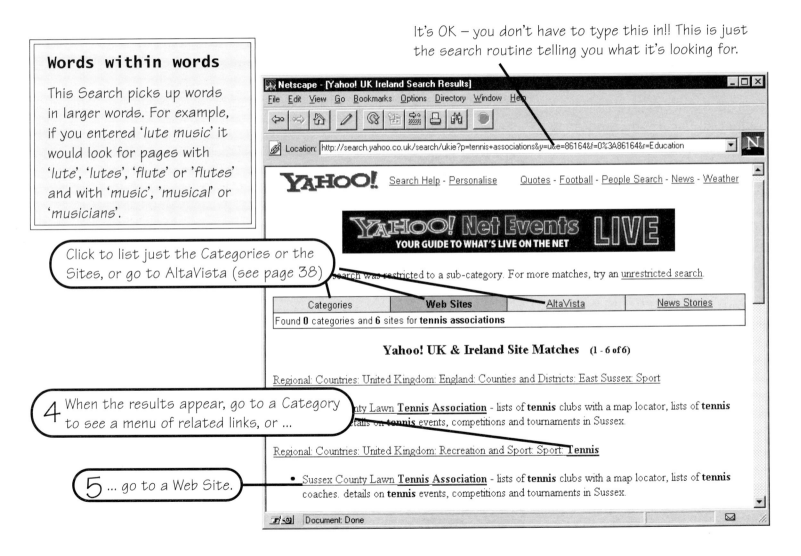

21

Lycos Top 5%

Lycos is one of the most popular sites on the Web – over 13 million people visit it every a day!

Its Top 5% Sites are rated on content and/or design, and each link is accompanied by a brief review. You won't find as many links here as at some directories, but they should be good ones.

Read the review before you go to a site, to check that it is likely to have what you are looking for.

Search for it!

You can search the Top 5% from here – just type a key-word and click Go Get It!

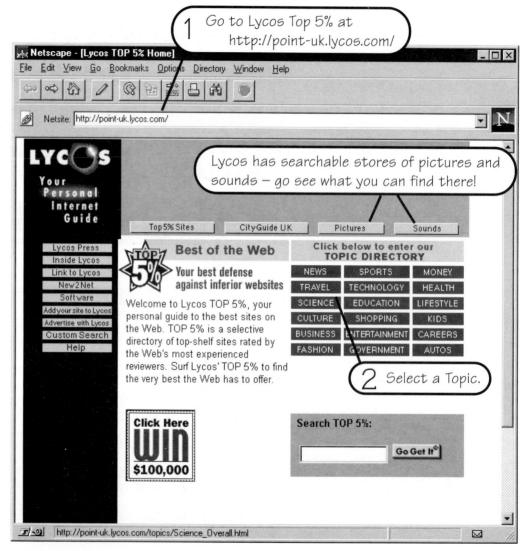

1 Go to Lycos Top 5% at http://point-uk.lycos.com/

Lycos has searchable stores of pictures and sounds – go see what you can find there!

2 Select a Topic.

Back into History!

If you want to go back to a directory, but have followed lots of links, open your History list and select the directory from there — it will be quicker that clicking the Back button. History is on the Window menu in Netscape, and a toolbar button in Internet Explorer.

The main Lycos site holds millions of links. If you can't find what you want in the Top 5%, you might like to try a search there. Lycos is at:

http://www.lycos.com

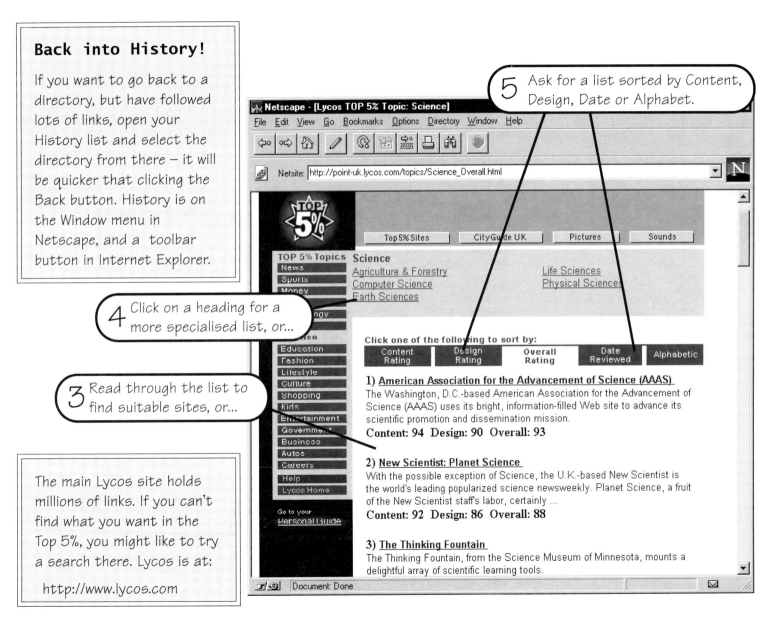

5 Ask for a list sorted by Content, Design, Date or Alphabet.

4 Click on a heading for a more specialised list, or...

3 Read through the list to find suitable sites, or...

UK directory

Tthe main Internet directories may not be the best place to look for stuff – simply because you will get too many irrelevant links. If you want local information, or local organisations or firms you are better off looking in a local directory.

The UK directory has links to UK businesses, shops, schools, colleges and government organisations, community groups, news, travel, entertainment and other services.

The directory is well organised, and you can probably find what you want by working through its menus. If not, you can easily run a search.

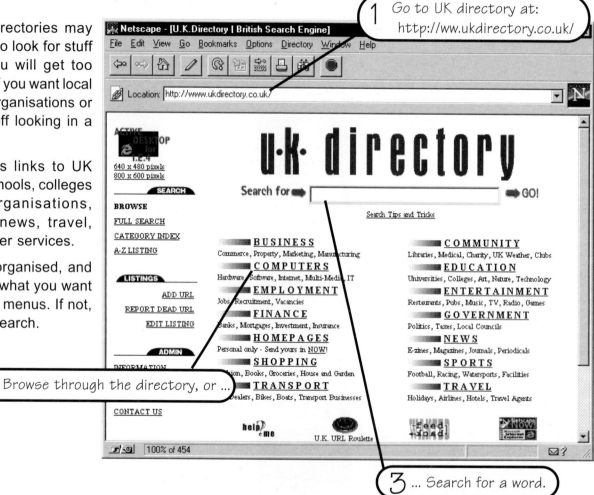

1 Go to UK directory at: http://ww.ukdirectory.co.uk/

2 Browse through the directory, or ...

3 ... Search for a word.

If a simple search doesn't find anything — or finds far too much — try the Full Search routine. This gives you a bit more control.

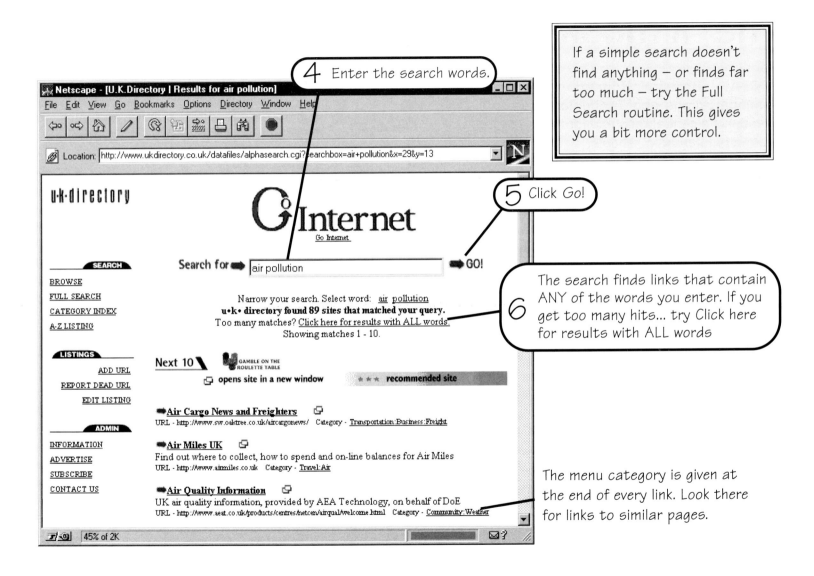

4 Enter the search words.

5 Click Go!

6 The search finds links that contain ANY of the words you enter. If you get too many hits... try Click here for results with ALL words

The menu category is given at the end of every link. Look there for links to similar pages.

25

The Window on the Web

BECTA (British Educational Communications and Technology Agency) is a central resource for the use of the Internet in schools.

Amongst other things, it holds good sets of links to educational resources on its **Window on the Web** page.

The Curriculum links are mainly for secondary schools (pupils and teachers). Some of the linked subject pages have more on them than others – English, Maths and Science have loads of links, while Music and Art have very few at the moment.

BECTA can be reached at:

http://www.becta.org.uk

BECTA was NCET (the National Council for Educational Technology) at the time of writing, but will have taken the new name by the time this is published. Expect the screens to look slightly different!

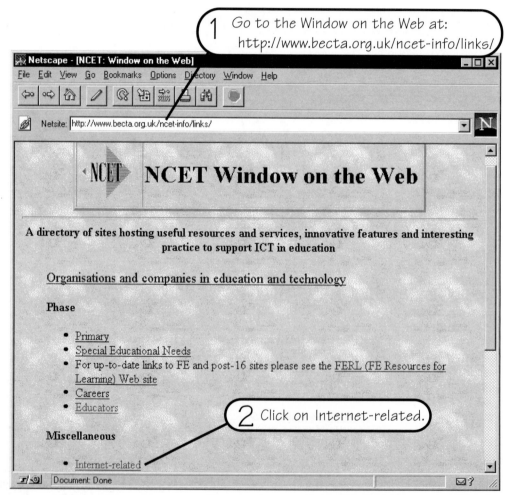

1 Go to the Window on the Web at: http://www.becta.org.uk/ncet-info/links/

2 Click on Internet-related.

There are more links further down the page!

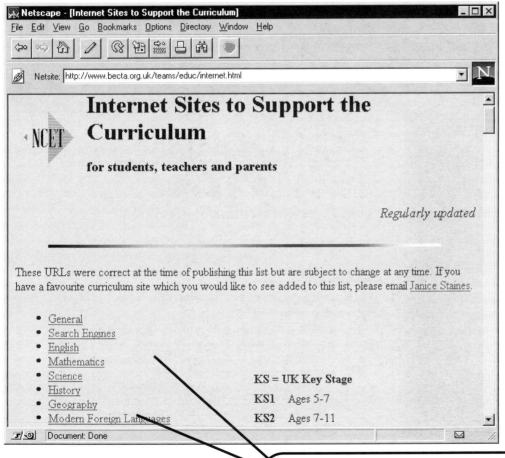

Homework Heaven

If you are looking for links to educational resources, you will probably find more in Homework Heaven than anywhere else on the Internet.

It is designed for US students, but its 300,000 links have been carefully selected and are well-organised.

Get to Heaven at:
http://www.homeworkheaven.com

3 Select a curriculum area then follow up the links on the subject pages

Tele-School OnLine

There are several organisations that hold sets of links to UK curriculum resources.

Some offer quantity – lots of links, but simply listed without comment. **Tele-School OnLine** takes this approach. Its links are well organised and cover all curriculum areas – some areas much better than others.

The Bookmarks are sets of other links which may be useful to schools.

The Tele-Café is area for teachers to swap ideas.

In any organisation's sets of links, expect some of them to be out of date – it is an impossible job to keep track of lots of links!

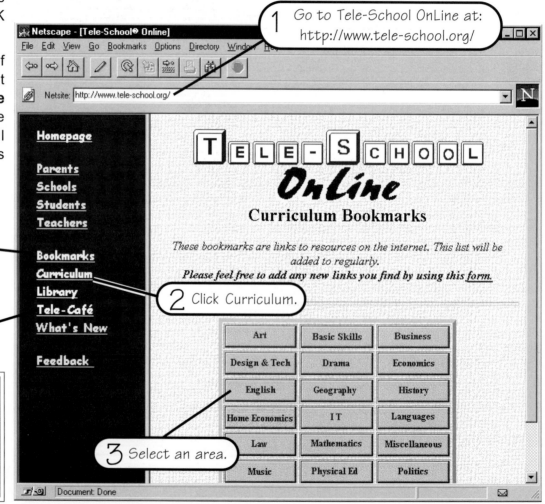

1 Go to Tele-School OnLine at: http://www.tele-school.org/

2 Click Curriculum.

3 Select an area.

Heinemann World

Heinemann World takes a different approach to links. There are fewer here than at Tele-School (though there are plenty), but each link is accompanied by a description of what you will find at the site. This tends to cut down time wasted visiting sites which turn out to be not what you expected.

1 Go to Heinemann World at: http://www.heinemann.co.uk/

Netscape - [First for Education: Subject Links]

File Edit View Go Bookmarks Options Directory Window Help

subject links

't miss... **Himalayas - where earth meets sky**
hensive site on the World Wide Web about the Himalayas.
high school students from three different continents for ThinkQuest (1997), an annual
enges students to use the Internet as a collaborative teaching and learning tool.

3 Select a curriculum area.

ence, life on earth, virtual
s and online experiments

- **Maths**
  online problems, interactive puzzles, challenging concepts and famous mathematicians

Languages
tionaries, French, German and esources

- **English Literature and Language**
  electronic texts, creative writing sites, children's literature reviews

phy
population, maps and more

- **The Environment**
  pressure groups, global resources and government information

from ancient to modern

- **Art**
  artists and their works, tips, techniques and children's artwork online

s, teaching tips and learning skills

t Done

Netscape - [Heineman

File Edit View Go Bookmarks Options Directory Window Help

Location: http://www.heinemann.co.uk/

N

Heinemann *World*
about...
first *for education*

REPP businesses access the information relevant to you... fast!

H Heinemann Educational
G GINN & Company
Rigby Education
Rigby Heinemann
B Butterworth Heinemann
H Heinemann USA
G Greenwood USA

pupils & students   teachers & librarians   parents   academics & professionals

http://www.reed-elsevier.com

2 Click (pictures or text) pupils & students or teachers & librarians.

WWW Virtual Library

The WWW Virtual Library is organised like the Window on the Web, but on a much larger scale. The main menus are kept up to date by Stanford University, but the subject pages are maintained by specialists scattered throughout the world. These people know and love their subjects and have assembled links to some of the best sites on the Web.

1 Go to the Virtual Library start page at http://vlib.stanford.edu/Overview2.html

Netscape - [WWW Virtual Library]

File   Edit   View   Go   Bookmarks   Options   Directory   Window   Help

Location: http://vlib.stanford.edu/Overview2.html

The WWW Virtual Library

- **Agriculture**
  Agriculture, Beer & Brewing, Gardening...

- **International Affairs**
  International Affairs, Sustainable Development, UN...

...Science
Graphics, Languages, Web...

- **Law**
  Law, Environmental Law

...ations and Media
...ons, Telecommunications, Journalism...

- **Industry and Economics**
  Economics, Finance, Transportation...

...ognitive Science, Libraries, Linguistics...

- **Recreation**
  Recreation, Collecting, Games, Sport...

...g
...l, Electrical, Industrial, Mechanical...

- **Regional Studies**
  Asian, Latin American, Middle East Studies...

...s
...istory, Museums, Philosophy...

- **Science**
  Biosciences, Medicine, Physics, Chemistry...

...n Management
...ciences, Knowledge Management...

- **Society**
  Political Science, Religion, Social Sciences...

Done

Netscape - [Virtual Library: Biosciences]

File   Edit   View   Go   Bookmarks   Options   Directory   Window   Help

Location: http://vlib.stanford.edu/Biosciences.html

The Virtual Library: Bio Sciences

- **Animal health, wellbeing, and rights**
  o Zoos
- Biochemistry
- Biodiversity and Ecology
- Biotechnology
- Biological Molecules
- Botany
- Developmental Biology
- Entomology
- Evolution

Document: Done

3 Work through the menus — maybe for two or three levels.

2 Scroll through the Overview and select a subject.

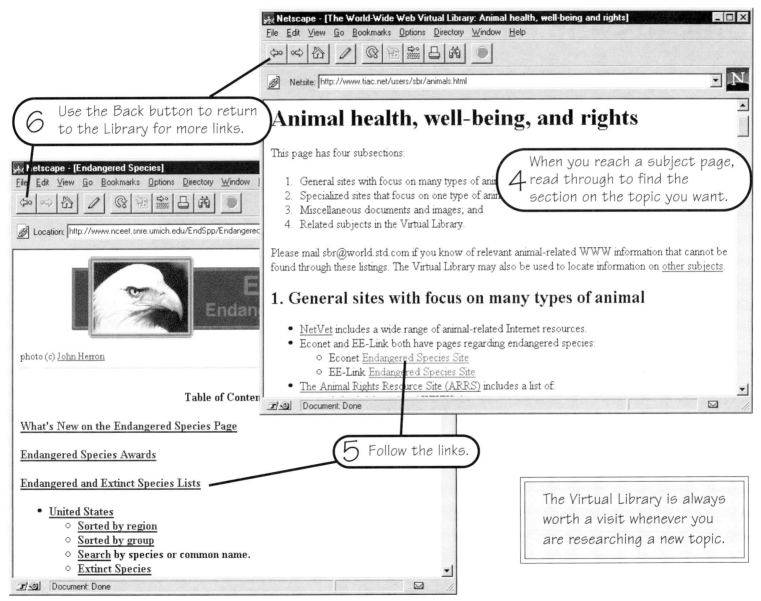

Use the Back button to return to the Library for more links. **6**

Netscape - [Endangered Species]
File Edit View Go Bookmarks Options Directory Window

Location: http://www.nceet.snre.umich.edu/EndSpp/Endangered

photo (c) John Herron

Table of Conten

What's New on the Endangered Species Page

Endangered Species Awards

Endangered and Extinct Species Lists

- **United States**
  - **Sorted by region**
  - **Sorted by group**
  - **Search by species or common name.**
  - **Extinct Species**

Netscape - [The World-Wide Web Virtual Library: Animal health, well-being and rights]
File Edit View Go Bookmarks Options Directory Window Help

Netsite: http://www.tiac.net/users/sbr/animals.html

Animal health, well-being, and rights

This page has four subsections:

1. General sites with focus on many types of ani
2. Specialized sites that focus on one type of ani
3. Miscellaneous documents and images; and
4. Related subjects in the Virtual Library.

When you reach a subject page, **4** read through to find the section on the topic you want.

Please mail sbr@world.std.com if you know of relevant animal-related WWW information that cannot be found through these listings. The Virtual Library may also be used to locate information on other subjects.

1. General sites with focus on many types of animal

- NetVet includes a wide range of animal-related Internet resources.
- Econet and EE-Link both have pages regarding endangered species:
  - Econet Endangered Species Site
  - EE-Link Endangered Species Site
- The Animal Rights Resource Site (ARRS) includes a list of:

Document: Done

5 Follow the links.

The Virtual Library is always worth a visit whenever you are researching a new topic.

Document: Done

31

CampusWorld

All the sites we've looked at so far have been open-access, free sites. They are run by government organisations as a public service, or by businesses as a way of encouraging people to look at what else they have to offer.

BT's CampusWorld is different. Small parts of it are open to non-members – so that you can see what you are missing – but most can only be accessed by subscribers.

Subscriptions costs £10 a month for single user access. If you want to be able to use CampusWorld from anywhere within a school network, you need a site license. The cost depends on the number of users – a typical secondary school would pay around £2,000 a year, though you do get more than just links for the money! There are a lot of good ideas here and opportunities for publishing your work, for joint projects and more.

Have a look at CampusWorld and see what you think.

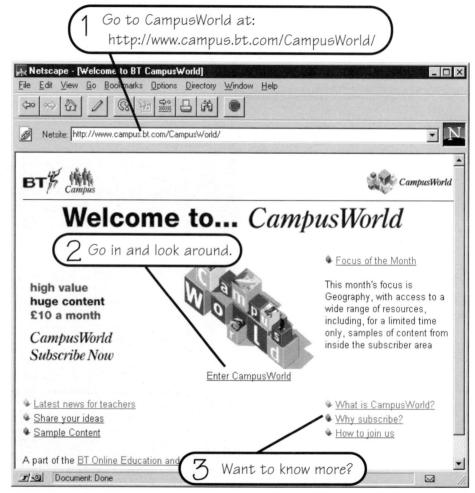

1 Go to CampusWorld at:
http://www.campus.bt.com/CampusWorld/

2 Go in and look around.

3 Want to know more?

CampusWorld has some good content. At the time of writing, a weather project was running in the Geography area. This included links to automatic weather stations around the UK, from which you could gather wind speed, temperature, rainfall, and other readings – updated every minute.

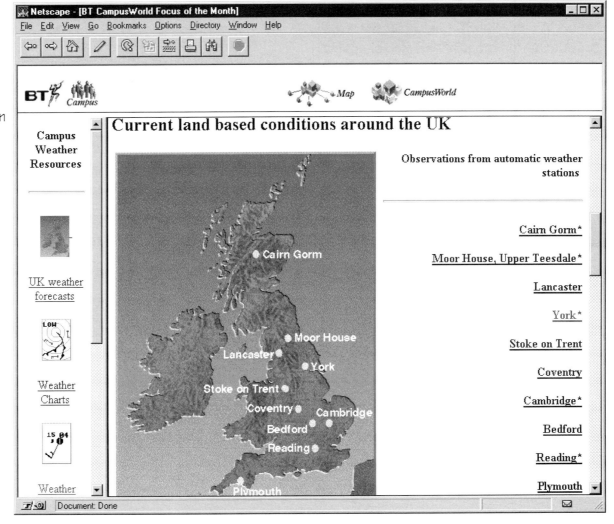

The Living Library

This is a new and growing service for subscribers to RM's EduWeb. It offers easy access to a wide range of selected or specially created material in all the main areas of the National Curriculum, along with news archives, resource packs, picture libraries and more general information sources.

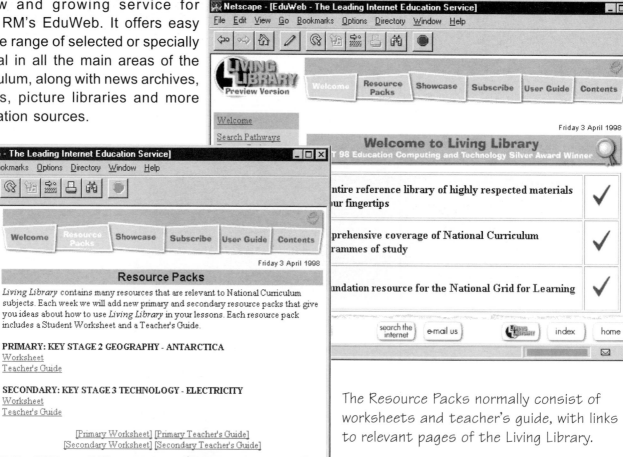

The Resource Packs normally consist of worksheets and teacher's guide, with links to relevant pages of the Living Library.

Pathways

Pathways has a great store of links to resources within local EduWeb and beyond. These can be searched, but if you are not sure which keywords to use, browsing is a better option. Each subject area has an A to Z list of keywords – selecting one of these brings up a list of relevant links.

The age range indicator, rating and summary will help you to decide which links are worth following up.

For more details of the Living Library, and to find out about joining, go to EduWeb at:

http://www.eduweb.co.uk

Things To Do

1 A company's Web address – its URL – is often the company's name, with **www** at the start and **com** or **co.uk** (for UK businesses) at the end. For example, Microsoft's URL is **http://www.microsoft.com**, Pepsi's URL is **http://www.pepsi.com** and the BBC's main site is at **http://www.bbc.co.uk**.

Use this pattern to find the Web sites of three well known companies.

2 Explore some other Web directories. See how they vary in the ways they select and organise their links, in how quickly and easily you can use them to find what you want. Here are a few you might like to try:

General:
Excite at **http://www.excite.com/**
Magellan at **http://www.mckinley.com/**
The Whole Internet Catalog at **http://gnn.com/gnn/**

UK:
UK Index at **http://www.ukindex.co.uk/**
Yell at **http://www.yell.co.uk/**

Schools:
Scottish Council for Educational Technology at **http://www.scet.org.uk/**
EduWeb at **http://www.eduweb.co.uk/**
(Go to the *Links* pages at both of these)

Links on-line

All the links given in this book can be found on-line at Heinemann World. Go to:

http://www.heinemann.co.uk/

and look for the schools' guide to the Internet.

3 Searching

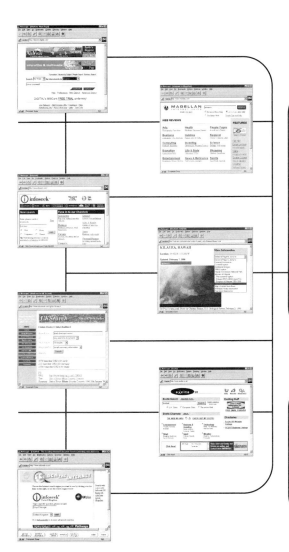

This chapter explores some search engines – places where you can go to search the Internet. They all work in much the same way – give them a word to look for and they will find pages that contain it – but they don't all reach the same corners of the Internet. When you are gathering material, it's always worth while trying several search engines.

AltaVista

Some people say that AltaVista is the king of the search engines. It's certainly very fast and has a huge database! Unless you are looking for something rare, a simple search can produce thousands of hits.

You don't want this many! To reduce the number – and to just get the stuff that you really want – you can the Advanced Search (page 41) or Refine the results. We'll try refining first.

In this example, the search is for information on Oliver Cromwell, with special reference to the Puritans and the Royalists. We start with 'oliver cromwell' as the first keywords.

> The Internet does not stay still for long! It is likely that some sites will have changed the details of their search routines by the time you get there – but the general approaches should still be the same.

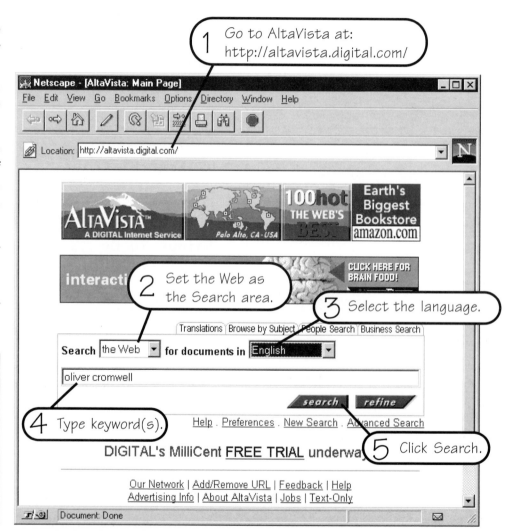

1 Go to AltaVista at:
http://altavista.digital.com/

2 Set the Web as the Search area.

3 Select the language.

4 Type keyword(s).

5 Click Search.

If you get a reasonable number of hits – enough, but not too many – follow the most likely links.

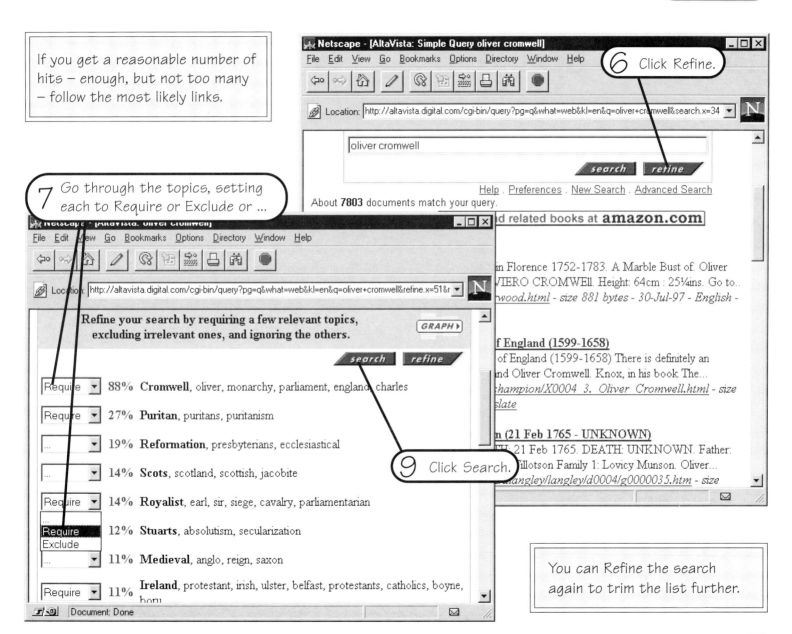

6 Click Refine.

7 Go through the topics, setting each to Require or Exclude or ...

9 Click Search.

You can Refine the search again to trim the list further.

Logical operators

At AltaVista (and most other search engines) you can use the operators AND, OR and NOT to link your keywords together.

AND

Every word must match to produce a hit, e.g.

fish AND chips

This will find the pages on traditional English food and nothing else. If you had used 'fish chips' without the AND, the search would also have found pages on sea creatures, microprocessors and much else besides.

OR

Either of the linked words will produce a hit, e.g.

egg OR fish AND chips

This will still find only food pages but with a wider menu. It is the same as doing two searches, one for 'egg AND chips', the other for 'fish AND chips'.

NOT

Ignore pages containing the following word, e.g.

fish AND chips NOT burgers

This makes it very traditional, avoiding places that do those new-fangled American things. (You might like to try this search, just to see what it does find!)

Names and phrases

If you are looking for a person's name or for a phrase, write it in "quotes". e.g.

"battered Mars bar"

This will only finds phrases that match exactly – it would not find 'Mars bar coated in crunchy batter'.

This works at almost all search engines.

Endings

Most search engines always look for plurals or other endings to words.

'**fish**' will also find '**fish**es', '**fish**y', '**fish**ed' and '**fish**ing'.

AltaVista doesn't normally do this. If you want it to look for alternative endings, add an asterisk (*) after the core word, e.g. fish*

> The operators can usually be written in either lower case or CAPITAL letters.

AltaVista's Advanced Search

You can use the logical operators in AltaVista's Advanced Search. You can also control the search in these ways.

◆ Link words with NEAR if they must be close together on a page.

◆ You can set date limits so that it only returns pages created between certain dates, or from a set date until now.

◆ If you enter words in the **Ranking** textbox, pages containing them will be listed first. This may not help much, as it tends to override the main search expression.

> 1 Type your keywords linking them with AND, OR, NOT or NEAR, if needed.

Netscape - [AltaVista: Advanced Query "Oliver Cromwell" AND Royalists AND Puri...]

File   Edit   View   Go   Bookmarks   Options   Directory   Window   Help

Location: http://altavista.digital.com/cgi-bin/query?pg=aq&what=web&kl=en&q=%22Oliver+Cromwell%22+

Translations Browse by Subject People Search Business Search

Search the Web ▼ for documents in English ▼

"Oliver Cromwell" AND Royalists AND Puritans AND Ireland

Ranking: Cromwell   From: 21/Mar/86   To:

☐ Give me only a precise count of matches.

search   refine

Help . Preferences . New Search . Simple Search

13 documents match your query.

Click to find related books at amazon

> 4 Click Search.

1. No Title
   The Project Gutenberg Etext of A Child's History of England** #11 in our series by Charles Dickens Copyright laws are changing all over the world, be sure.
   http://www.ul.cs.cmu.edu/gutenberg/etext96/achoe10.txt - size 929K - 14-Mar-97 - English - Translate

Document: Done

> 2 Enter the most crucial keywords in the Ranking textbox.

> 3 Set the dates if the age of the material matters.

Magellan

Magellan has two unique features. First, it has a database of **Green Light** sites – ones that will be acceptable at school and in the family home. (It also has a database of 60,000 reviewed and 50 million unreviewed sites.)

The second is **concept-based searches** – when it finds documents, it 'reads' them and learns which words and ideas are associated with one another. So, if you search for 'movies', it will also look for 'video', 'films', 'cinema' and similar.

Search words

With a simple list of words, Magellan will look for pages containing any of them, but put those that contain all – or most – at the top of the results list.

You can use the operators AND, OR and AND NOT to link words. These must be written in CAPITALS.

WEB REVIEWS is a directory of Magellan's reviewed sites.

1 Go to Magellan at: http://www.mckinley.com/

2 Enter your search word(s) or expression.

Find similar

If your keywords have several meanings, the first set of hits may cover a range of topics.

To focus on the ones you want, read through to find the most suitable result and click on its **find similar**. This is the concept-based searching in action! In the example, the search on 'amazon' found material on the river in Brazil, as well as stuff on parrots, the bookshop, sushi (!) and other irrelevancies. (And if it hadn't been restricted to Green light sites, it would also have found feminist and girlie pages.)

The **find similar** link by the Amazon home page turned up a wealth of material on the river basin – the object of the search.

3 Select the area to search – Reviewed sites, Green Light sites or the Entire Web.

4 Click search.

5 Scroll through and view the results or ...

6 ... click find similar for more pages on the same topic.

43

Infoseek

Infoseek is a great place to find stuff! It searches through the text of over 30 million pages, and it offers an unusual, but brilliantly simple, way to search the Internet. When you get a set of results, you can search through those results – and keep on doing that – so that you focus in on what you want. Instead of struggling to write one complex search expression, you simply give another defining word or set of words at each stage.

In the example, I'm looking for photographs of volcanoes in Hawaii, using the search words 'volcano', then 'Hawaii' and finally 'photo'.

◆ If you give several words, Infoseek will try to match any of them – e.g. 'mule donkey ass' will find any long-eared beast of burden.

◆ If you are searching for people, capitalise the names – e.g. 'Bill Gates' will find references to the man; 'bill gates' will find pages on birds, accounts, logic chips and garden entrances.

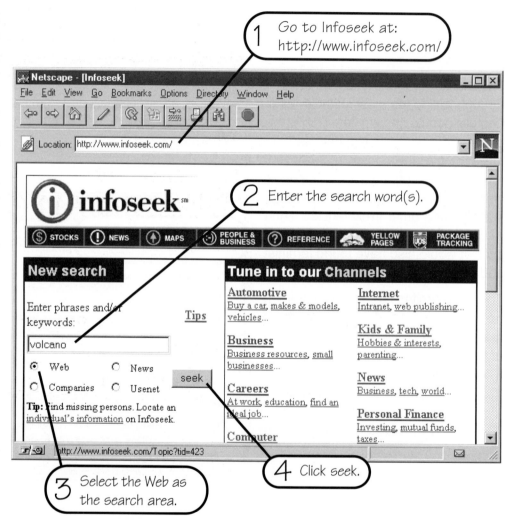

1 Go to Infoseek at: http://www.infoseek.com/

2 Enter the search word(s).

3 Select the Web as the search area.

4 Click seek.

- If you really want to, you can write search expressions containing logical operators – read the Tips at Infoseek to find out how.

- You can also search through the latest News stories, or through the Usenet newsgroups, or for company information on nearly 50,000 firms in the US.

'Related topics' are probably not related after the first level!

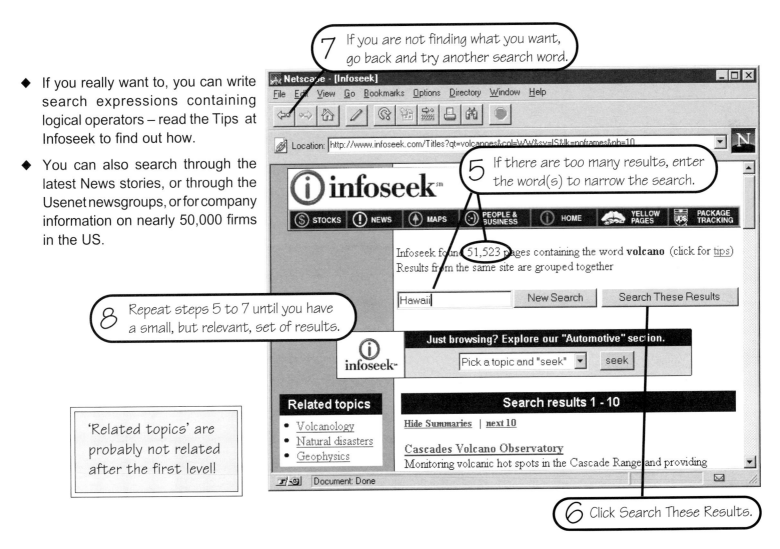

7 If you are not finding what you want, go back and try another search word.

5 If there are too many results, enter the word(s) to narrow the search.

8 Repeat steps 5 to 7 until you have a small, but relevant, set of results.

6 Click Search These Results.

After three levels of searches, I'm down to 77 hits — almost all relevant — and there were some great photos at one of the first sites in the list.

UK Search

The UK Search database has links to around 250,000 sites, which is not that many compared to Infoseek, but these are all in the UK. If you are looking for a club or a company or an organisation and it is important that they are in the UK – start here.

Search options

These are rather limited. You can choose whether to look in the title, heading, text or all of each document. You can also set the style and number of the results display.

When searching, it will try to match any of the words, but list first those that contain all of them – if there is no good stuff in the first page of results, don't bother to look at the next.

> The operators AND, OR and NOT do not work here.

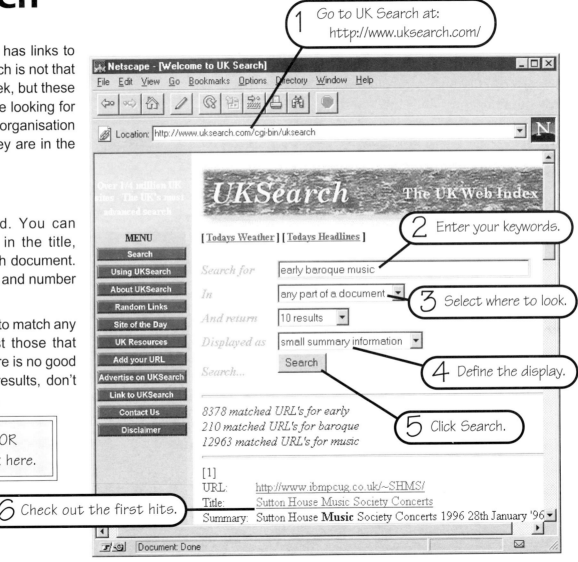

1 Go to UK Search at:
http://www.uksearch.com/

2 Enter your keywords.

3 Select where to look.

4 Define the display.

5 Click Search.

6 Check out the first hits.

Excite UK

Excite's search facility is only one of the services that it provides to the Internet. There is also a catalogue, which contains probably the most comprehensive set of **reviewed** sites on the Web. These brief, but thoughtful, reviews make this one of the best places to start browsing.

When entering your search words, you can link them by AND – if you want all the words to be matched – or OR if a match on any word will do.

A useful feature of Excite is that you can limit the search to UK or European sites, as well as searching the whole Web.

You can also search at the main Excite site at:

http://www.excite.com/

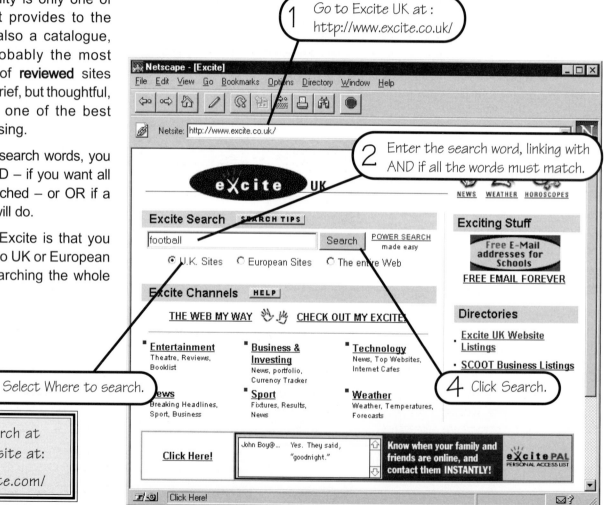

1 Go to Excite UK at :
http://www.excite.co.uk/

2 Enter the search word, linking with AND if all the words must match.

3 Select Where to search.

4 Click Search.

Refining a search

While Excite is searching, it builds a list of words that crop up regularly on the pages that it finds. The most common ones are then listed at the top of the search results. You can use these to filter your results. Just select those words that relate to your topic (they will be written into the search box for you), and click **Search** again.

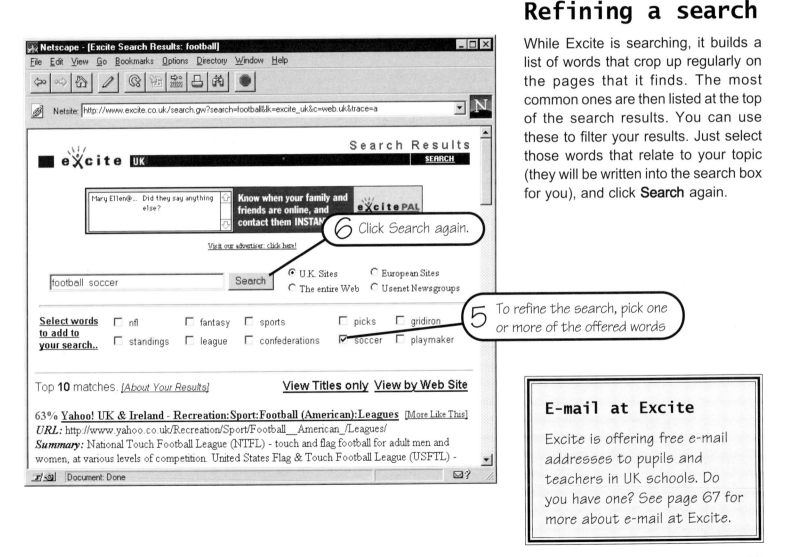

6 Click Search again.

5 To refine the search, pick one or more of the offered words

E-mail at Excite

Excite is offering free e-mail addresses to pupils and teachers in UK schools. Do you have one? See page 67 for more about e-mail at Excite.

Eduweb's one-stop search

Sometimes you will have to try several different search engines before you get the results you want. That's when you really appreciate places like Eduweb. Their Search the Internet page lets you search six of the best search engines and directories – without having to go to any of them.

In the example, I was looking for information on Lloyd George, the great Liberal Prime Minister. The first try at Yahoo was no use – all it found was a company in Hong Kong. The next try was at Infoseek and that came up with three hits. The first of these was exactly what I wanted – an excellent exhibition at the National Library of Wales.

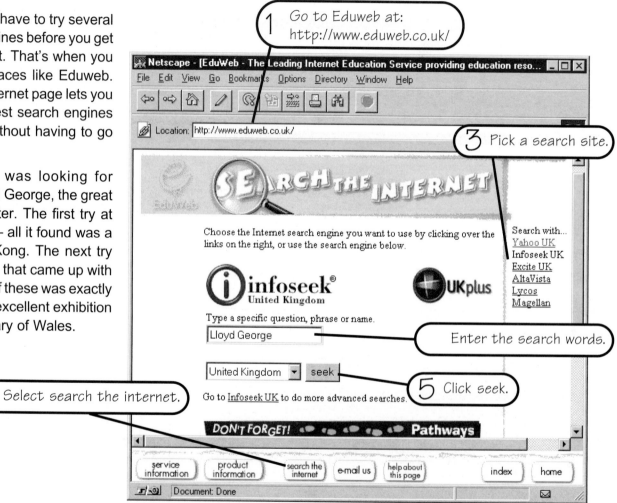

1 Go to Eduweb at: http://www.eduweb.co.uk/

3 Pick a search site.

Enter the search words.

2 Select search the internet.

5 Click seek.

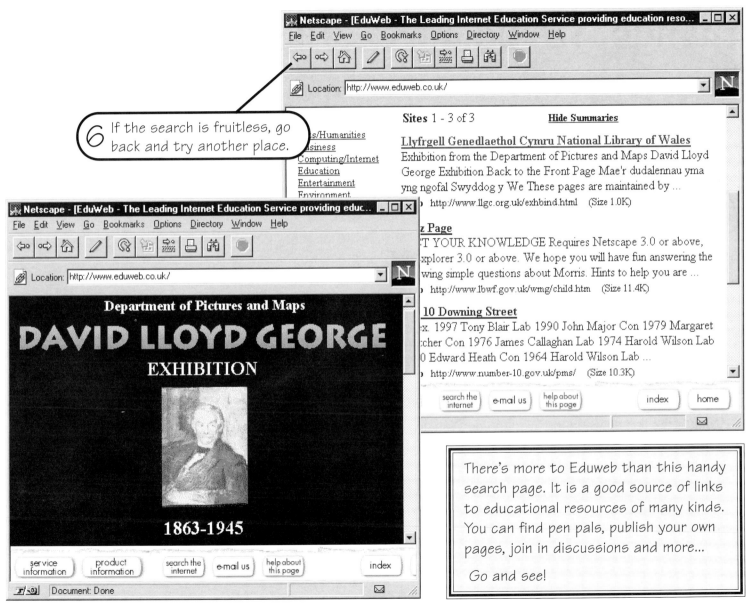

6 If the search is fruitless, go back and try another place.

Netscape - [EduWeb - The Leading Internet Education Service providing education reso...

File Edit View Go Bookmarks Options Directory Window Help

Location: http://www.eduweb.co.uk/

s/Humanities
siness
Computing/Internet
Education
Entertainment
Environment

Sites 1 - 3 of 3   **Hide Summaries**

Llyfrgell Genedlaethol Cymru National Library of Wales
Exhibition from the Department of Pictures and Maps David Lloyd George Exhibition Back to the Front Page Mae'r dudalennau yma yng ngofal Swyddog y We These pages are maintained by ...
http://www.llgc.org.uk/exhbind.html   (Size 1.0K)

z Page
'T YOUR KNOWLEDGE Requires Netscape 3.0 or above, xplorer 3.0 or above. We hope you will have fun answering the wing simple questions about Morris. Hints to help you are ...
http://www.lbwf.gov.uk/wmg/child.htm   (Size 11.4K)

10 Downing Street
ex. 1997 Tony Blair Lab 1990 John Major Con 1979 Margaret cher Con 1976 James Callaghan Lab 1974 Harold Wilson Lab 0 Edward Heath Con 1964 Harold Wilson Lab ...
http://www.number-10.gov.uk/pms/   (Size 10.3K)

search the internet | e-mail us | help about this page | index | home

Netscape - [EduWeb - The Leading Internet Education Service providing educ...

File Edit View Go Bookmarks Options Directory Window Help

Location: http://www.eduweb.co.uk/

Department of Pictures and Maps

DAVID LLOYD GEORGE

EXHIBITION

1863-1945

service information | product information | search the internet | e-mail us | help about this page | index

Document: Done

There's more to Eduweb than this handy search page. It is a good source of links to educational resources of many kinds. You can find pen pals, publish your own pages, join in discussions and more...

Go and see!

Things To Do

1 Test several search engines to see which produce most results and which find things faster. Look for words that you would expect to find on lots of pages, such as 'graphics', 'software', 'sport', 'music', etc.

The time it takes to get the results is affected by the amount of traffic on the Internet between you and the search engine. This varies all the time. You will get a better idea of the speed of a search engine if you repeat the same test several times and work out the average time.

2 See which search engines are best for finding more obscure things. Look for unusual musical instruments, specialist scientific terms, lesser-known writers or historical figures.

Is any one engine better at these than the rest, or does it depend upon the kind of information you are looking for?

3 Use the Internet to find out more about the Internet.

What are Gopher, FTP and telnet?

Who is or was Alan Turing, Marc Anderssen, John Junod?

What is the link between the World Wide Web and CERN?

Search at the school's guide on-line

The search engines covered in this chapter can be reached from the guide's on-line page at:
http://www.heinemann.co.uk/

4 Sites to see

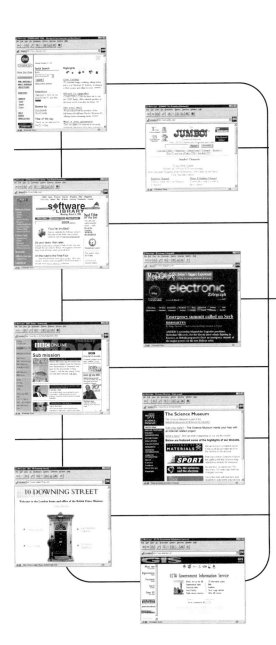

The World Wide Web has – literally – millions of sites to see. Here is just a tiny selection to give you an idea of some of the kinds of sites that you may find worth visiting.

Shareware sites

One of the great things about the Internet is that you can get from it the software that you need to get the best out of it. Much of it is free, and most of the rest is low-cost **shareware** – try it for free, but pay the (small) fee if you are going to carry on using it.

There are lots of sites with shareware for downloading. Three of the best are covered in the next few pages.

shareware.com

shareware.com has literally megabytes of shareware (and freeware). There are areas that you can browse, but it is normally best to use the Search routine. This looks for a match in the names and in the descriptions of the programs.

If you are just starting to build a shareware collection, have a look through the Most Popular section.

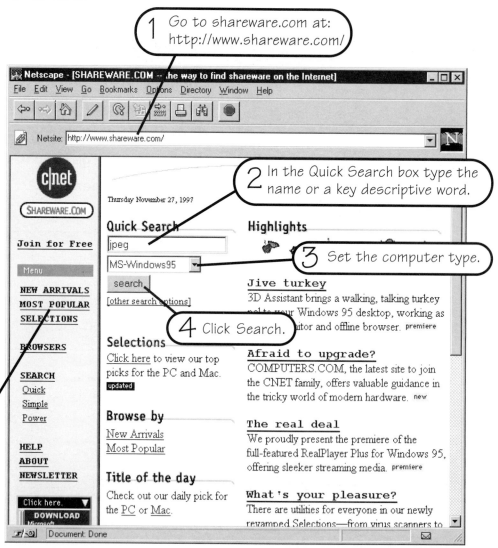

1 Go to shareware.com at: http://www.shareware.com/

2 In the Quick Search box type the name or a key descriptive word.

3 Set the computer type.

4 Click Search.

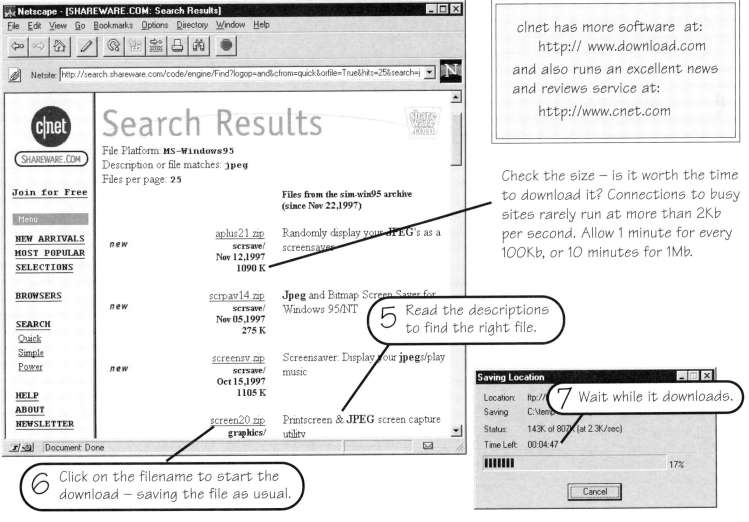

clnet has more software at:
http:// www.download.com
and also runs an excellent news
and reviews service at:
http://www.cnet.com

Check the size – is it worth the time to download it? Connections to busy sites rarely run at more than 2Kb per second. Allow 1 minute for every 100Kb, or 10 minutes for 1Mb.

5 Read the descriptions to find the right file.

6 Click on the filename to start the download – saving the file as usual.

7 Wait while it downloads.

55

Shareware at Jumbo

Jumbo started up in mid-1995, with the aim of becoming the biggest and best shareware site on the Net. By early 1998, it had over 250,000 files at the tip of its trunk – and was still growing fast.

The files are grouped into 'channels', then into topic within the channels, plus there are special areas including *Top Downloads* and *Starter Kits*. Browsing here or in the channels is probably the best way to find software at Jumbo.

There is a search routine, but it is not that good – it will only find programs where you have given the name or a word that is used in its brief description.

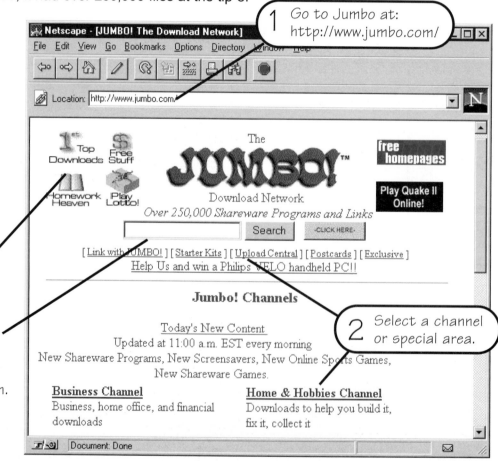

1 Go to Jumbo at:
http://www.jumbo.com/

2 Select a channel or special area.

Find the most popular software in Top Downloads.

To search, type the name of the program or a word you might expect to find in its description, then click Search.

Scroll down for lots more channels

The Software Library

This is hosted by ZDNet, one of the Internet's great content providers. The Software Library offers quality, rather than quantity, though over a wide area.

It's an excellent place to get the tools you need for work on the Internet or for enhancing your computer system, and has a good selection of children's software and animated images.

The Software Library is at:

http://www.hotfiles.com

The mainZDNet site is at:

http://www.zdnet.com

1. Go to the Software Library at: http://www.hotfiles.com/

2. Select an area and browse its files.

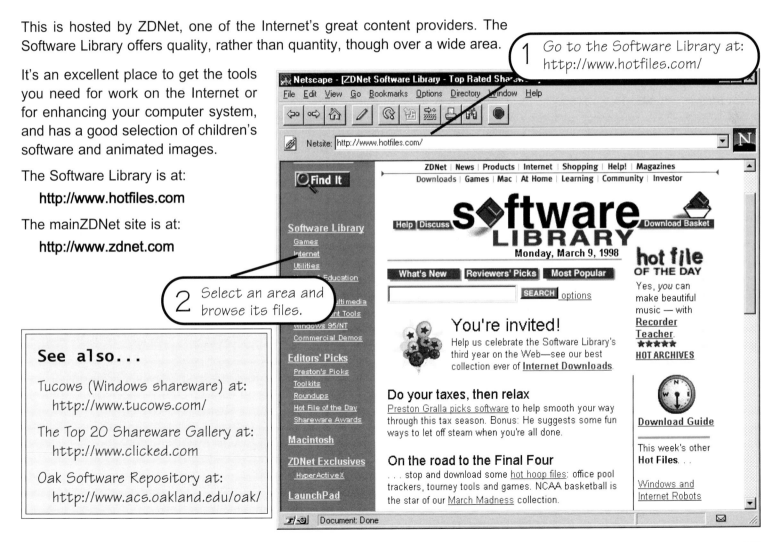

See also...

Tucows (Windows shareware) at:
    http://www.tucows.com/

The Top 20 Shareware Gallery at:
    http://www.clicked.com

Oak Software Repository at:
    http://www.acs.oakland.edu/oak/

Media

The Telegraph was the first to go 'electronic'.
Read it at: http://www.telegraph.co.uk/

Newspapers and television have long been used as sources of information and stimulus in a range of subjects. Now that many have their own Web sites, they are even more valuable.

Newspapers

Newspapers on the Web have a number of advantages over the printed versions.

◆ You don't have to buy 30 copies for a whole class to be able to read the same – or different – articles at the same time.

◆ If you want to use pictures or quotes from text in an essay, they can be copied directly from the screen into a word-processor.

◆ Papers often have searchable archives so that you can research stories from past issues.

Most papers insist that you to register before letting you into the site. There's normally no charge – they just like to know who's reading them.

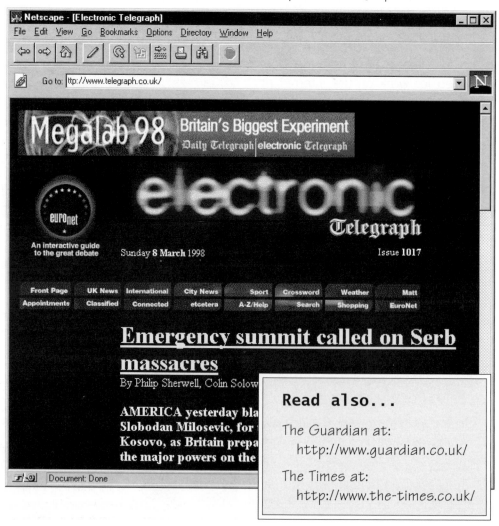

Read also...

The Guardian at:
http://www.guardian.co.uk/

The Times at:
http://www.the-times.co.uk/

Television

Over the last year or so, the BBC has put a great effort into developing their Web site, with excellent results.

BBC Online has a magazine format, with lots of snippets to lead you into its main stories. The rest of the BBC's extensive site can be reached from here, or use the URLs to go to:

The News at:
http://www.bbc.co.uk/news

The Education service at:
http://www.bbc.co.uk/education/

Don't miss the Bitesize GCSE revision guides at:
http://www.bbc.co.uk/education/bitesize

View also...

Channel 4 at:
http://channel4.co.uk/

The Computer Channel
http://www.computerchannel.co.uk

To find your local ITV station, go to http://www.ukdirectory.co.uk and work through the menus Entertainment > TV > TV channels.

Museums and galleries

All the main museums and art galleries – and some of the smaller ones – in the UK and most other countries, are now on the Internet. Their Web sites can be used in two main ways:

If the museum is within travelling distance of your school, you can find out about opening times, special exhibits, costs, etc. to plan your visits.

More distant places can be 'visited' through the Web. It's rarely as good as actually being there, but it's better than nothing.

MuseumNet has a comprehensive listing of UK museums, with links for those that are on the Web, and other contact information for the rest.

MuseumNet is at:

http://www.museums.co.uk

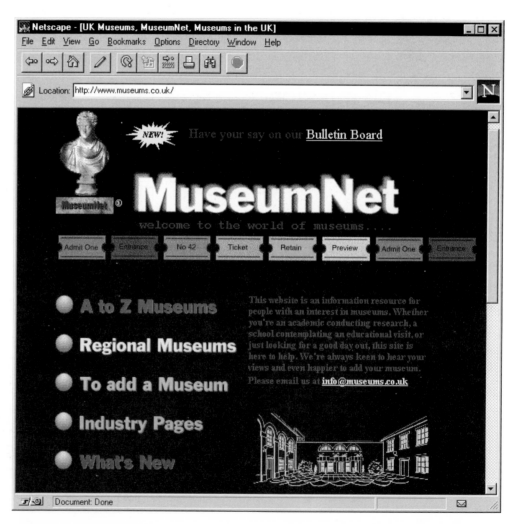

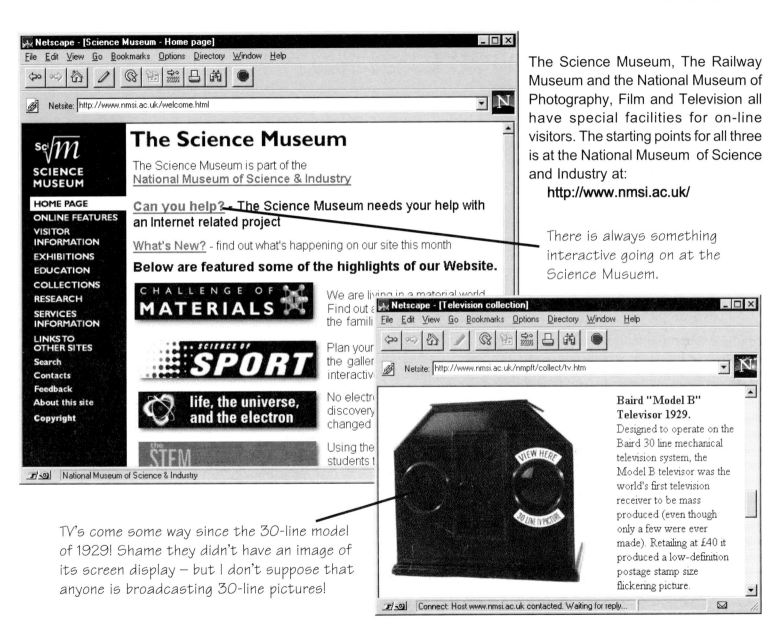

The Science Museum, The Railway Museum and the National Museum of Photography, Film and Television all have special facilities for on-line visitors. The starting points for all three is at the National Museum of Science and Industry at:

http://www.nmsi.ac.uk/

There is always something interactive going on at the Science Musuem.

TV's come some way since the 30-line model of 1929! Shame they didn't have an image of its screen display – but I don't suppose that anyone is broadcasting 30-line pictures!

Baird "Model B" Televisor 1929.
Designed to operate on the Baird 30 line mechanical television system, the Model B televisor was the world's first television receiver to be mass produced (even though only a few were ever made). Retailing at £40 it produced a low-definition postage stamp size flickering picture.

Open government

New Labour, new Web sites! Two years ago, the British government did not seem to know that the Internet existed. Now just about every department and government service has its Web site, to tell people about its work, to publish papers and research findings, and as the focus of two-way communication with the public.

The main site is run by the Governement Information Service, and is found at:

http://www.open.gov.uk

If you are studying politics, law or the constitution, this is an obvious resource, but it is also useful in many other areas of study. Any serious work on the economy, environment or education (or just about any other current issue) could benefit from a visit.

How about a virtual tour of Number 10?
And don't forget to sign the Visitors'
Book before you leave!
The PM lives at:
http://www.number-10.gov.uk

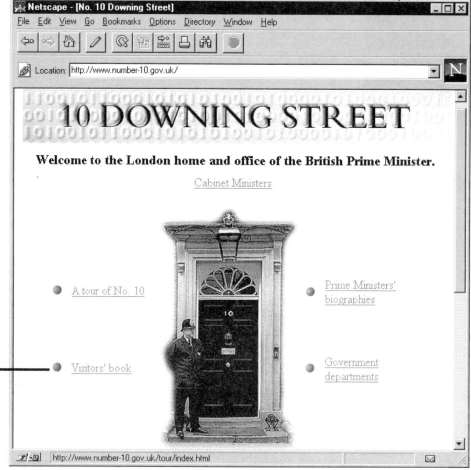

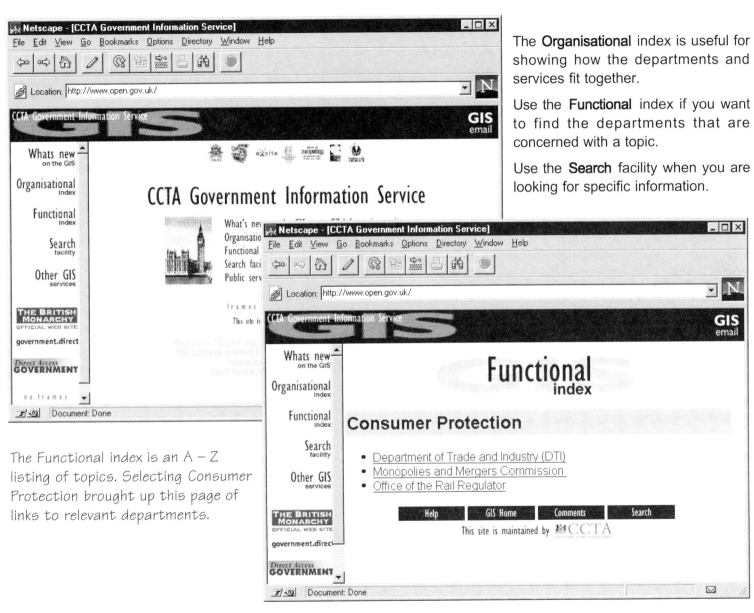

The **Organisational** index is useful for showing how the departments and services fit together.

Use the **Functional** index if you want to find the departments that are concerned with a topic.

Use the **Search** facility when you are looking for specific information.

The Functional index is an A – Z listing of topics. Selecting Consumer Protection brought up this page of links to relevant departments.

63

Things To Do

1 Find out what your school policy is on downloading and installing software. What space is available, and where? If shareware is dowloaded, who is responsible for paying the registration fee if it goes into use?

If software can be downloaded, one of the first things you will need is a decompression program, as most files are compressed for faster transfer. The best decompressors are:

Stuffit Expander (for Windows or Apples) from Aladdin Systems at **http:www.aladdinsys.com**

WinZip(for Windows) from Nico Mak Computing at:**http://www.winzip.com**

2 Find out if your local newspapers and radio stations are on the Web. They may be listed at the UK Directory or Yahoo UK.

3 Use the Web to plan a trip to a museum or art gallery – it need not be close by, as you can easily find times and costs of international travel through the Web.

Find your flights at Yahoo Travel (**http://travel.yahoo.com**).

The schools' guide on-line

The links given in this guide are all available on-line at Heinemann World at: http://www.heinemann.co.uk/schoolguide.htm

---

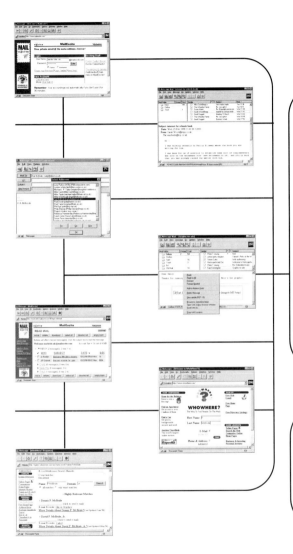

5 E-mail

E-mail is a great way to keep in touch with old friends — and to make new friends!

If you don't know your e-mail address, or don't know what software to use, or haven't yet got an address, talk to your teacher or technician before reading this chapter.

Electronic mail

E-mail is the simplest, cheapest and quickest way to keep in touch with distant friends and family, and to exchange ideas with other schools in this country and overseas – as long as they are also on the Internet. An e-mail message can:

◆ be as long or short as you like – some systems set a limit of 1000 lines, but that is unlikely to be a problem!

◆ have pictures, documents or other files attached to it;

◆ be sent to many people at once;

◆ be forwarded on from one person to another, with added comments;

◆ be written and read off-line – you only need to be on-line to get and send mail.

The mail will sometimes get through almost at once, but at worst it will be there in a few hours. Your message will pass through several computers before it reaches the other end, and these do not hand each message on immediately. Instead, they connect to each other at regular intervals to deal with the mail.

E-mail addresses

The standard pattern for a person's e-mail address is:

username@service.provider   (@ is said 'at')

There are some variations to the pattern. Here are some of the names that I have had while researching this book. **TCP** follow the standard pattern.

macbride@tcp.co.uk

CompuServe give their members numbers, rather than names – though once you have joined, you can arrange a 'proper' name for yourself as well.

100407.2521@compuserv.co.uk

Address Books

You must type e-mail addresses exactly right or they won't work. Fortunately, you should only have to type it once for each person.

Almost every mail system has an Address Book file where you can store addresses. Find your Address Book now and learn how to use it.

E-mail and Web e-mail

E-mail is not delivered – you have to get it from your mailbox. But where is your mailbox, and does it matter where it is?

Normal e-mail

If you get your mail through your access provider – the organisation that links your school to the Internet – your mailbox is on their mail server (a computer at their site).

To collect or send mail:

1   Logon to the Internet.

2   Run your mail software (or open the Mail window of your browser).

3   Give the Get Mail or Send Mail command.

You do not need to be on-line to read or create messages.

Web e-mail

If you have a Web e-mail connection (probably at Excite), your mailbox is on a computer on the Web.

1   Logon to the Internet.

2   Run your browser and go to the Web e-mail site.

3   Login and read your mail or write and send new mail.

You must be on-line to read or create messages.

MailExcite

Excite is offering free e-mail addresses to pupils and staff in UK school.

Web e-mail has one big advantage over normal e-mail. Your user name and e-mail address is separate from your normal login name. If you change schools, or want to get or send mail from home or from a public terminal (e.g. in your local library), you can still use the same MailExcite mailbox.

Pupils who already have an e-mail account through school, must check with their teachers before signing up with MailExcite.

Use a word-processor

In any e-mail system, you can save messages as files and read them in a word-processor.

You can word-process your messages then copy-and-paste them into the mail window, or send them as attached files (see page 74).

Getting an Excite mailbox

Follow the steps shown here. Don't forget to Bookmark the page before you leave, so that you can get back to it easily.

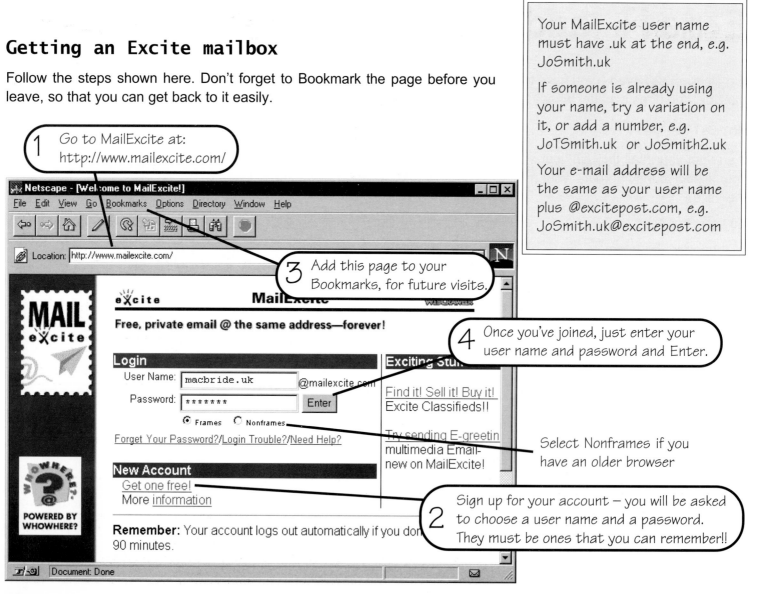

Your MailExcite user name must have .uk at the end, e.g. JoSmith.uk

If someone is already using your name, try a variation on it, or add a number, e.g. JoTSmith.uk or JoSmith2.uk

Your e-mail address will be the same as your user name plus @excitepost.com, e.g. JoSmith.uk@excitepost.com

1 Go to MailExcite at: http://www.mailexcite.com/

3 Add this page to your Bookmarks, for future visits.

4 Once you've joined, just enter your user name and password and Enter.

Select Nonframes if you have an older browser

2 Sign up for your account – you will be asked to choose a user name and a password. They must be ones that you can remember!!

Reading the mail

Before you can read your mail, you have to get it – the postman does not deliver on the Internet!

If you get your mail through your service provider, run your e-mail software and use its **Get new mail** (or similar) command.

If you use MailExite, go to the site and login – any new mail will be in your inbox already.

When you get new messages, you will see their header lines in your inbox. These show who sent the mail, when it was sent and what its subject is.

Click (double-click on some systems) on the header line to read the message.

Messages stay in your inbox until you move them or delete them – time I cleared mine out!

The sender's e-mail address is always shown. Most mail systems have an easy way to add the address to your Address Book.

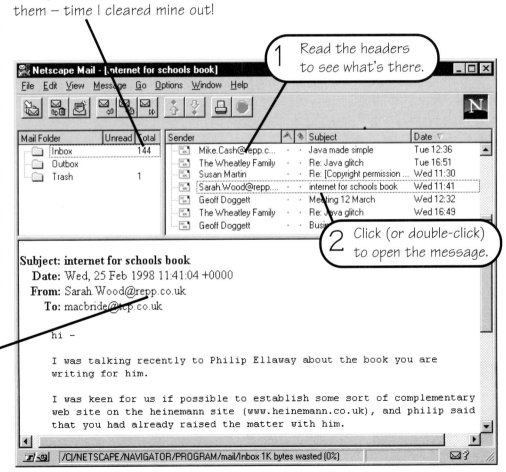

Read the headers to see what's there.

Click (or double-click) to open the message.

69

Sending messages

To send e-mail, all you need is the address – and something to say! Messages can be composed and sent immediately if you are on-line, or composed off-line and stored for sending later.

Who to?

To send a message to one person, simply type their address (or pick it from your Address Book) into the To: slot.

If you want to send the message to several people at once, you can do this in two ways.

Either:

Write the addresses into the **To:** slot, separated by commas, e.g.

To: fbloggs@net.co.uk, jgreen@school.net

Or:

Write the other addresses into the **Cc:** (Carbon copies) slot. Everyone who gets the mail will be able to see who the message was sent **To** and who else has had copies.

Some systems allow you to send **Bcc** (Blind carbon copies). With these, no-one can see who else had copies of the mail.

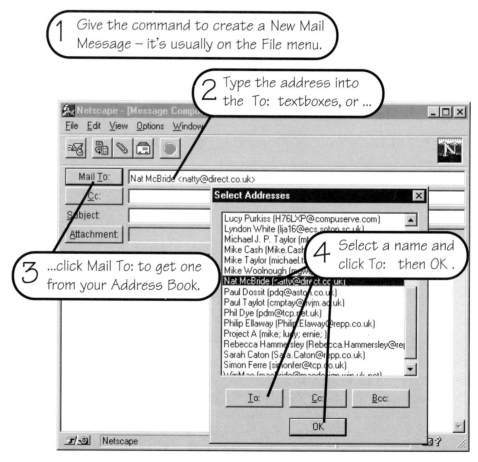

1 Give the command to create a New Mail Message – it's usually on the File menu.

2 Type the address into the To: textboxes, or ...

3 ...click Mail To: to get one from your Address Book.

4 Select a name and click To: then OK .

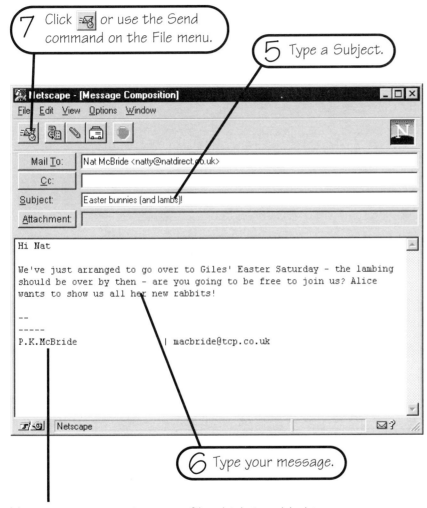

7 Click ✉ or use the Send command on the File menu.

5 Type a Subject.

6 Type your message.

You can create a signature file which is added to the end of all your messages. Mine simply has my name and e-mail address. Some people include favourite quotes or create pictures with characters.

Subject lines

Subject lines are important as they help your recipients to organise their messages. Make them brief, but clear. People read the Subject lines of incoming mail, to see which to deal with first – and which to ignore completely! They also need the Subjects when organising old mail, so that they know which to delete and which to place in what folder.

Emphasis

If your recipient's Mail system can handle formatted text, then you can use <u>underline</u>, **bold** or *italics* for emphasis. If you are sending plain ASCII text, and want to make a word stand out, enclose it in *asterisks* or _underscores_, or write it in CAPITALS.

Don't shout!

MESSAGES TYPED ALL IN CAPITALS ARE TIRING TO READ (aren't they!).

Typing in capitals is known as 'shouting' in the jargon of the Net.

Replying

When you reply to an incoming message, the system will open the Compose window and copy the sender's address into the To: slot.

◆ The Subject will also have been copied in, but with Re: tacked on the front.

◆ The original message may have been copied into the message with > at the start of each line (or may not – it depends on the options on your system). This can be very handy if you want to respond to the mail point-by-point. You can insert your text between the lines, and any unwanted lines can be deleted.

◆ If you want the sender's address, copy it now, and paste it into your Address Book. The e-mail address is normally shown in <angle brackets> after the sender's real name.

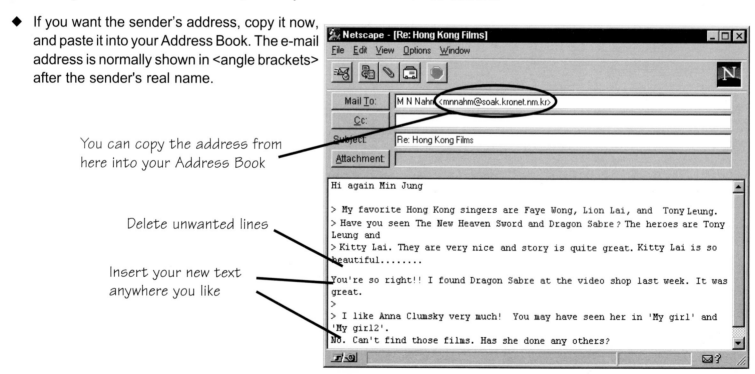

You can copy the address from here into your Address Book

Delete unwanted lines

Insert your new text anywhere you like

Forwarding

If you receive a mail and want to send it on to another person, you can forward it. This is very like replying to a message, except that you need to give the next person's e-mail address.

Smileys and Abbreviations

Smileys

E-mail messages tend to be brief, and as your recipients cannot see your expression or hear the tone of your voice, you may be misunderstood – especially when you are joking.

Smileys, also known as *emoticons,* are little pictures, composed of ASCII characters (the ones you can see on your keyboard), that can help to convey your meaning.

The basic smiley of **:–)** is the one you will see most often, though there are many other weird and wonderful smileys around. A few of the more common ones are shown here.

:-)	It's a joke
'-)	Wink
:-(	I'm feeling sad
:-o	Wow!
:-C	I don't believe it!
(-:	I'm left handed
%-)	I've been staring at a screen for hours!
8-)	I'm wearing sunglasses

Abbreviations

If you are a slow typist, or like to keep your messages short, or are likely to be getting mail from old 'netties', then it's worth learning a few of the standard abbreviations. You will also find these used in real-time chat lines, and in newsgroup articles.

```
Hi Jake

WRT the best browser. IMHO you can't beat Netscape,
but I'd be interested to see the new one for the
Acorn. Can you tell me where I can get a copy?

TIA

Sally
```

BTW	By The Way
FYI	For Your Information
IMHO	In My Humble Opinion (jokingly)
POV	Point Of View
TIA	Thanks In Advance
TTFN	Ta Ta For Now
WRT	With Reference To
<g>	Grin

Files by mail

Files of any type – graphics, word-processed documents, audio and video clips – can be attached to messages and sent by e-mail. This is almost always quicker and cheaper than sending them printed or on disk in the post. But, the larger the file, the longer it takes to get through, and the greater the chance of errors. Somewhere over 1 megabyte, the time you and your recipient spend on-line will start to outweigh the postage costs.

The **As Is** option may not work. Some people's e-mail software will not be able to cope with files in their original form. If you have tried As Is and the file didn't get through, use the **Convert to Plain Text** option and try again. All e-mail software can handle plain text.

Here's how to send files using Netscape's Mail window. The routine is much the same from other mail software.

1 Start to create a new message as normal.

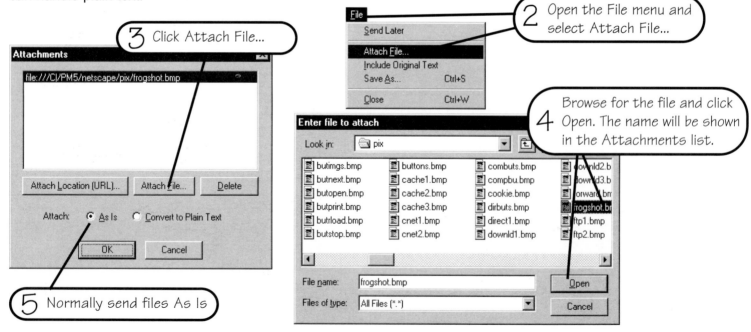

2 Open the File menu and select Attach File...

3 Click Attach File...

4 Browse for the file and click Open. The name will be shown in the Attachments list.

5 Normally send files As Is

Incoming files

When you get mail with an attached file, you can deal with it in several ways:

◆ If your mail software can display the file, it will. GIF and JPG graphics will be displayed in the message, and HTML documents in a new window.

◆ If the browser cannot display it, you will see a note or an icon to show that there is an attached file. If you click on this (or right-click on it to open the shortcut menu and select the **Browse** or **View** option) it should run the application to display it. PCX and BMP graphics, Word documents and plain text files can usually be viewed this way.

◆ If the browser knows of no means of viewing the file, you will get an **Unknown File Type** message. Use the **Save File** option and hunt out a suitable application later – you can find viewers for almost every type of file on the Internet.

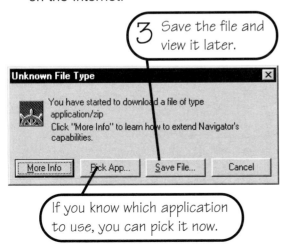

3 Save the file and view it later.

If you know which application to use, you can pick it now.

1 Click to view the file, or...

2 Right-click and use the Browse option.

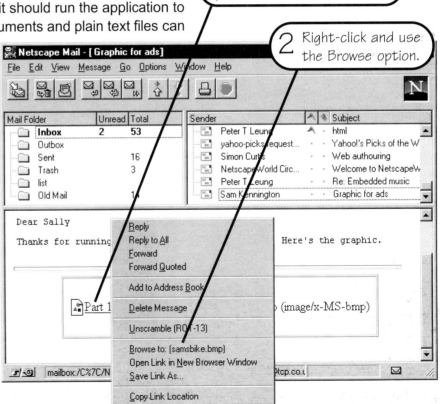

75

Using MailExcite

Sending and reading mail through a Web page is almost the same as doing it with the mail software on your computer. There are a few small differences.

◆ You can only read or create and send message when you are on-line. If you want to be able to read a message off-line, you must download it, or copy it and paste it into a word-processor file on your computer.

◆ To read a message, click on its Subject.

◆ Everything is done in the same window. When you have finished reading a message, or have written and sent a message, **don't close the window** – use the **Back** button to return to the main display.

◆ Messages are stored in your area at MailExcite until you remove them. You are allocated lots of space, but it will fill up eventually! The **Delete** button moves messages to the 'Trash' folder. You must click **Empty Trash** to clear them completely.

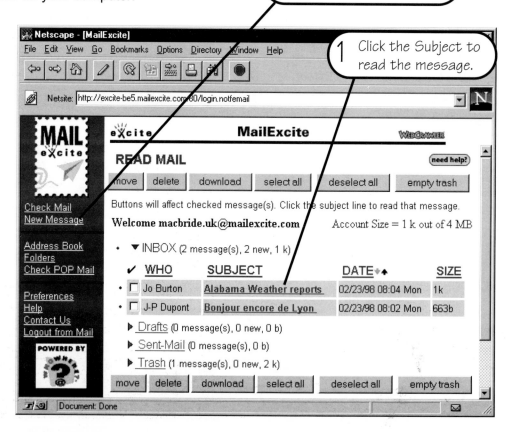

4 Click New Message when you want to send mail.

1 Click the Subject to read the message.

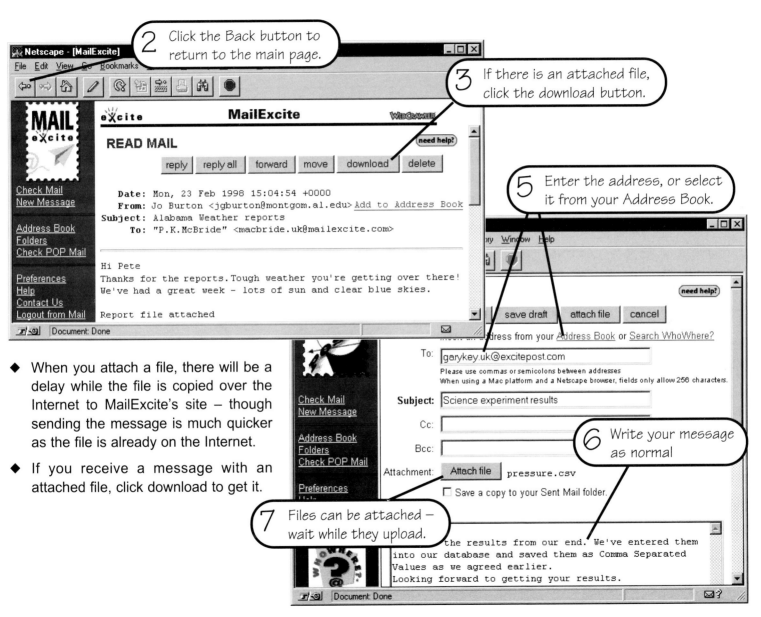

2 Click the Back button to return to the main page.

3 If there is an attached file, click the download button.

5 Enter the address, or select it from your Address Book.

Netscape - [MailExcite]

File Edit View Go Bookmarks

e**X**cite   **MailExcite**   WEBCRAWLER

READ MAIL   (need help?)

reply   reply all   forward   move   download   delete

Date: Mon, 23 Feb 1998 15:04:54 +0000
From: Jo Burton <jgburton@montgom.al.edu> Add to Address Book
Subject: Alabama Weather reports
To: "P.K.McBride" <macbride.uk@mailexcite.com>

Hi Pete
Thanks for the reports. Tough weather you're getting over there!
We've had a great week – lots of sun and clear blue skies.

Report file attached

Document: Done

save draft   attach file   cancel

...dress from your Address Book or Search WhoWhere?

To: garykey.uk@excitepost.com
Please use commas or semicolons between addresses
When using a Mac platform and a Netscape browser, fields only allow 256 characters.

Check Mail
New Message

Address Book
Folders
Check POP Mail

Preferences

Subject: Science experiment results

Cc:

Bcc:

Attachment: Attach file   pressure.csv

☐ Save a copy to your Sent Mail folder.

6 Write your message as normal

7 Files can be attached – wait while they upload.

...the results from our end. We've entered them
into our database and saved them as Comma Separated
Values as we agreed earlier.
Looking forward to getting your results.

Document: Done

◆ When you attach a file, there will be a delay while the file is copied over the Internet to MailExcite's site – though sending the message is much quicker as the file is already on the Internet.

◆ If you receive a message with an attached file, click download to get it.

Finding e-mail addresses

Test a directory by looking for yourself or for someone else you are sure is on-line.

There is no central Internet address book. So, if you want to send e-mail to people, how do you find their address?

The simplest solution is to get them to send you e-mail. Their address will be on the message.

If you are trying to find long-lost friends or relatives, there are 'people-finding' places on the Internet. These have databases of e-mail addresses, though they do not cover everybody.

WhoWhere?

This is probably the best people-finder. It's quick, easy-to-use and seems to have more addresses than its competitors.

● First names can be written in different ways – full names, initials, nicknames. Even last names do not follow strict rules – are you sure of the spelling?

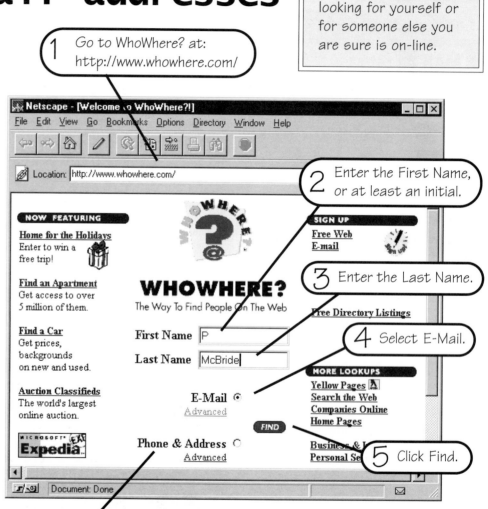

1 Go to WhoWhere? at: http://www.whowhere.com/

2 Enter the First Name, or at least an initial.

3 Enter the Last Name.

4 Select E-Mail.

5 Click Find.

Phone & Address only finds people in the USA

WhoWhere? - refining the search

Common names will produce far too many hits – you must find some way of restricting the search. The standard search looks for an **exact match**, and finds those which contain the given names – looking for 'P McBride', finds 'P K McBride' or 'Peter McBride' as well as any other McBride whose name started with 'P' or had 'P' as a middle initial.

If **all matches** is selected, 'P McBride' will also find any 'MacBride' and 'McBride' with different initials.

You can restrict a search to a **domain**. This could be the name of the service provider, if known, e.g. 'compuserve' or 'RMPLC'. Outside of the USA, give the country code as the domain.

Country	Domain code
UK	uk
France	fr
Germany	gr
Ireland	ie
Italy	it
Spain	sp
Australia	au
Canada	ca

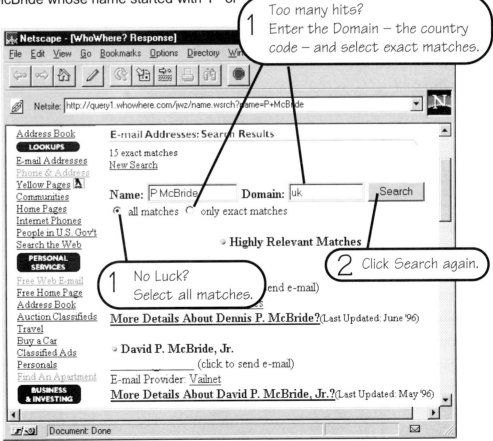

1 Too many hits?
Enter the Domain – the country code – and select exact matches.

1 No Luck?
Select all matches.

2 Click Search again.

79

Things To Do

1 Work with a partner within your school on this. Check that you are using your e-mail software properly by sending each other a simple message. When you receive the message, send a reply.

2 Repeat exercise **1** sending messages with attached files. Are you able to detach and view the file that you receive?

3 See if you can find a distant friend or relative – or yourself – at WhoWhere? Other people-finders you can try are:

Bigfoot at:　　http://www.bigfoot.com

Infospace at: http://www.infospace.com

Find them at the school's guide on-line

There are links to people finders on the guide's on-line page at: http://www.heinemann.co.uk/

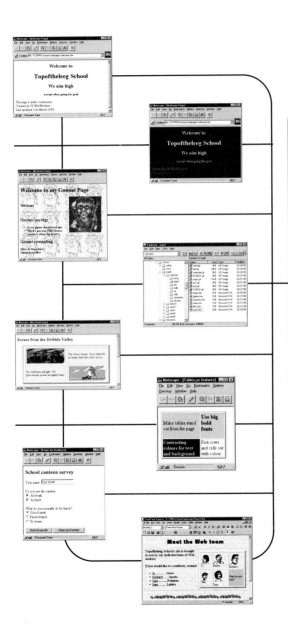

6 Creating a Web site

Creating a simple, but effective, Web site is not difficult, and most of the tools that you need to do the job are probably already at hand. This chapter introduces some of the ideas and techniques that you need to know to create a Web site for your school.

The school site

Why have a Web site?

In today's connected world, a Web site can play a key role in a school's communications with the outside world – *and within the school.* It can:

◆ Keep parents and pupils informed about events at the school.

◆ Exhibit pupils' individual and class work.

◆ Tell prospective parents (and staff!) what the school has to offer.

◆ Act as a resource centre, holding organised sets of links to useful sites.

What special about Web sites?

When planning your site, bear these things in mind:

◆ Web sites are far more flexible than paper publications, such as newsletters. Pages are not laid out in a fixed order but can be linked so that readers can take different routes through the site. The pages are not fixed in size. Screen-length pages are easier for visitors to handle, but if the page has to be screens (or more) long – it can be.

◆ In a printed paper you can tell your readers about things happening elsewhere – in a Web site you can add the links that will let your readers go elsewhere to see for themselves.

◆ Publication is not a once-and-for-all matter. You should expect to update your site regularly, editing, removing or adding pages.

What goes on a Web site?

You might include:

About the school

Information for pupils (or staff) thinking of joining the school

Staff links

League table figures

Special features

News and events

Calendar for the term/year

Sports results

Individual achievements

Plays, concerts, fêtes, etc.

Pupils' pages

Class projects

Individual home pages

Resources

In-school topic pages

Useful links

Publishing within the school

You don't *have* to publish your site on the World Wide Web. In fact, it is a good idea not to do that at first. Start by making the site available just within the school. This is easy to do, and gives those involved – and the rest of the school – a chance to test the links, spot mistakes and suggest improvements.

To publish your site within the school, all you need to do is store the files in a place where everyone can get at them.

◆ If you have a network, they should be stored in a public directory.

◆ If the computers are not linked, put the site files onto the computer in the library or other open-access area.

Publishing on the World Wide Web

When you are ready to show your site to the world, you must upload all the files to your access provider's server – a computer that they have linked permanently into the Web. Uploading is easiest if you have Netscape, Internet Explorer or FrontPage, which all have publishing 'wizards'. Without these, you will need special software for transferring your files.

Exactly where and how you upload the files is something that the teacher or technician responsible for the site should sort out with the access provider.

Back up!!

Always keep a safe backup copy of your Web site files. And whenever you add to or edit the files, make a new copy of the whole set. It will only take a few minutes and may save you days of frustration!

First on the Web!

Hinchingbrooke School in Cambridgeshire was the first UK school on the Web. Its site shows what a school can do. Go and see at:

http://edweb.camcnty.gov.uk/hinchingbrooke

HTML basics

HTML – HyperText Markup Language – is the system used to produce Web pages. It is a set of tags (codes) that set text styles, draw lines, display images, handle URL links and the other features that create Web pages. It is not hard to learn. There are only a limited number of tags and they follow fairly strict rules.

All tags are enclosed in <angle brackets> and are normally used in pairs – one at the start and one at the end of the text that they affect. For example:

```
<H1> This is a main heading </H1>
```

Notice that the closing tag is the same as the opener, except that it has a forward slash (/) at the start.

All pages have the same outline structure:

```
<HTML>
<HEAD>
   <TITLE>Welcome Page</TITLE>
</HEAD>
<BODY>
   Welcome to my home page
</BODY>
</HTML>
```

The whole text is enclosed by **<HTML>** and **</HTML>** tags.

The **<HEAD>** area holds information about the page, and is not displayed – though the Title does appear in the browser's Title bar when loaded. This can be left blank.

The **<BODY>** area is where the main code goes.

Writing HTML

HTML documents can be produced on any word-processor – they are only text files. For browser to recognise that they are HTML pages, the files must have an .HTM or .HTML extension.

On a PC, this is just a matter of adding the extension when you save the file. The top page, for example, might be named '**main.htm**'.

On an Acorn, start your browser before creating the file in the editor. After you have saved the file, use the Set Type option to set it to HTML.

HTML editors

These make it easier to write Web pages.

If you are working on a PC, try Netscape's Editor (page 104) or FrontPage (page 106).

There are also some good shareware editors. Go to **http://shareware.com** (page 54) and see what's on offer.

Set up a new directory for your home page files and keep everything in one place.

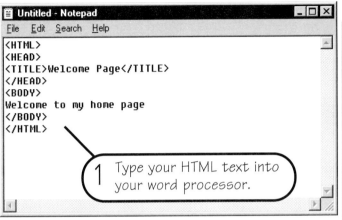

1 Type your HTML text into your word processor.

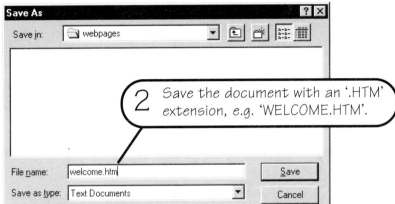

2 Save the document with an '.HTM' extension, e.g. 'WELCOME.HTM'.

The Title appears here

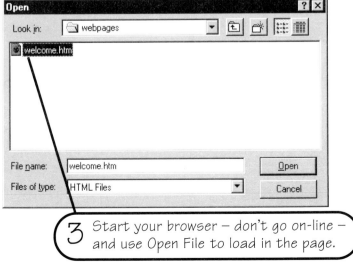

3 Start your browser – don't go on-line – and use Open File to load in the page.

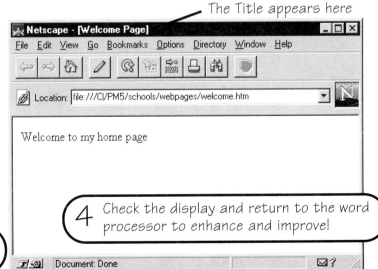

4 Check the display and return to the word processor to enhance and improve!

Working with text

The simplest tags are the ones that format text. These will produce six levels of headings, a small, italicised style (mainly used for e-mail addresses), and bold and italic for emphasis.

```
<H1>        </H1>        Heading 1 (Largest)
<H2>        </H2>        Heading 2
<H3>        </H3>        Heading 3
<H4>        </H4>        Heading 4
<H5>        </H5>        Heading 5
<H6>        </H6>        Heading 6 (Samllest)
<B>         </B>         Bold
<I>         </I>         Italic
<Address>   </Address>  Small italic style
```

The Heading and Address tags break the text up into separate lines, but untagged text appears as a solid block – no matter how you lay it out in your word processor.

Create separate paragraphs with these tags:

```
<P>     Start a new paragaph with a space above
</P>    End of paragraph (optional)
<BR>    Line break - no space before the new line.
        This is a single tag. There is no </BR>
```

When a browser reads an HTML document, it ignores all spaces (apart from a single space between words), tabs and new lines. What this means is that it doesn't matter how you layout your HTML text. You can indent it, and add line breaks to make it easier for you to read, but it won't affect what your readers see – only the tags affect the layout of the page in the browser.

Alignment

Text is normally aligned to the left, with a ragged edge on the right – like this paragraph. If you want your headings, or any other text, aligned down the centre of the page, use the **<CENTER>** tag. Notice that it's spelled the American way!

Font size

Ordinary text – not headings – can be defined using the **<FONT>** tag. This can takes several options, one of which is **SIZE**. The tag:

```
<FONT SIZE = 1>
```

sets following text to be very small. For the biggest possible text use:

```
<FONT SIZE = 7>
```

When you set a **<FONT...>** option, it stays in place until you turn it off with a closing **</FONT>** tag, or a new **<FONT ...>** option.

Look out for the **SIZE** setting in the example on page 90.

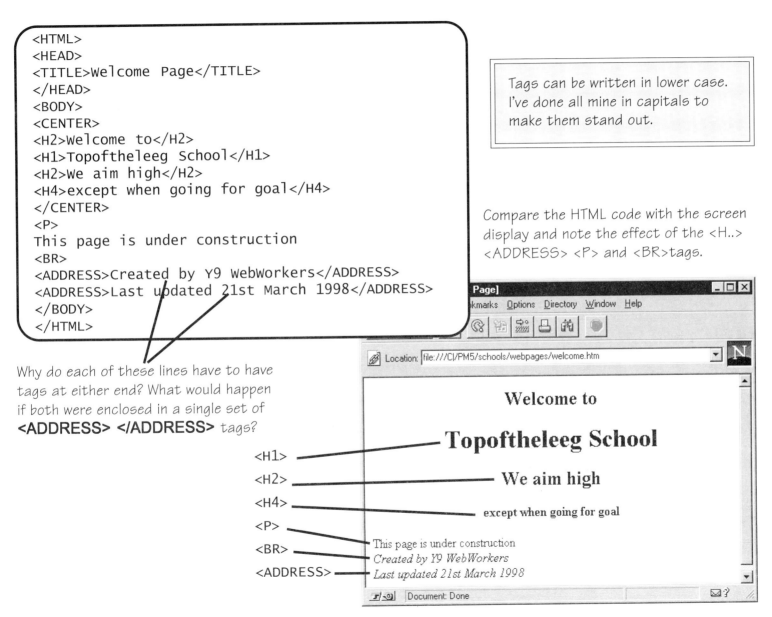

```
<HTML>
<HEAD>
<TITLE>Welcome Page</TITLE>
</HEAD>
<BODY>
<CENTER>
<H2>Welcome to</H2>
<H1>Topoftheleeg School</H1>
<H2>We aim high</H2>
<H4>except when going for goal</H4>
</CENTER>
<P>
This page is under construction
<BR>
<ADDRESS>Created by Y9 WebWorkers</ADDRESS>
<ADDRESS>Last updated 21st March 1998</ADDRESS>
</BODY>
</HTML>
```

Tags can be written in lower case. I've done all mine in capitals to make them stand out.

Compare the HTML code with the screen display and note the effect of the <H..> <ADDRESS> <P> and
tags.

Why do each of these lines have to have tags at either end? What would happen if both were enclosed in a single set of **<ADDRESS> </ADDRESS>** tags?

Page]

kmarks Options Directory Window Help

Location: file:///C|/PM5/schools/webpages/welcome.htm

Welcome to

Topoftheleeg School

<H1>

We aim high

<H2>

except when going for goal

<H4>

This page is under construction

<P>

Created by Y9 WebWorkers

Last updated 21st March 1998

<ADDRESS>

Document: Done

Using colour

Text-only pages are fast to load, but can be a bit boring. Colour will add impact to your screens, without adding to the loading time.

BODY colours

The colours of the background and text of the page can be set by including the **BGCOLOR** and **TEXT** options in the **BODY** tag.

    <BODY BGCOLOR = White TEXT = Green>

The background of the whole page will now be white – you can't change it further down – and all the text will be green unless you change it in the <FONT> tag.

FONT COLOR

At any point on the page, you can set the colour of the text with the tag:

    <FONT COLOR = ColorName >

The colour is used for text until a **</FONT>** tag restores the original **TEXT** colour or another **<FONT COLOR = ... >** tag sets a new colour.

You can use it to pick out words within normal text – though you can get strange results if you use the tags inside Headings.

> Note those US spellings
> – 'COLOR' and 'Gray'

Colour names

Browsers recognise certain names for colours – here are the main ones:

Black	Gray	Silver
White	Navy Blue	Blue
Green	Lime	Maroon
Red	Turquoise	Purple
Olive	Aqua	Fuchsia
Orange	Yellow	

Colour names can be written in lower case or capitals.

> You can set your own colours by defining how much Red, Green and Blue should be used, but you have to use hexadecimal numbers and many browsers can only show the limited colours given above. Keep things simple – use the colour names.

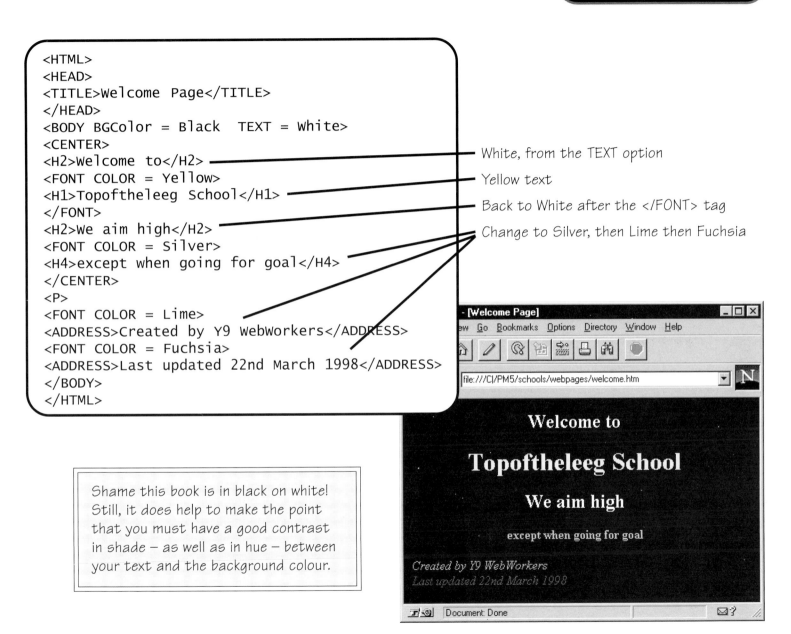

```
<HTML>
<HEAD>
<TITLE>Welcome Page</TITLE>
</HEAD>
<BODY BGColor = Black   TEXT = White>
<CENTER>
<H2>Welcome to</H2>
<FONT COLOR = Yellow>
<H1>Topoftheleeg School</H1>
</FONT>
<H2>We aim high</H2>
<FONT COLOR = Silver>
<H4>except when going for goal</H4>
</CENTER>
<P>
<FONT COLOR = Lime>
<ADDRESS>Created by Y9 WebWorkers</ADDRESS>
<FONT COLOR = Fuchsia>
<ADDRESS>Last updated 22nd March 1998</ADDRESS>
</BODY>
</HTML>
```

White, from the TEXT option

Yellow text

Back to White after the </FONT> tag

Change to Silver, then Lime then Fuchsia

Shame this book is in black on white! Still, it does help to make the point that you must have a good contrast in shade — as well as in hue — between your text and the background colour.

- [Welcome Page]

ew Go Bookmarks Options Directory Window Help

file:///C|/PM5/schools/webpages/welcome.htm

Welcome to

Topoftheleeg School

We aim high

except when going for goal

Created by Y9 WebWorkers
Last updated 22nd March 1998

Document: Done

89

Lists

Lists come in two varieties: Ordered Lists (numbered) and Unordered Lists (bulleted). Both types are set up in the same way. Here's the basic shape:

```
<OL>
  <LI> List item </LI>
  <LI> List item </LI>
  <LI> List item </LI>
</OL>
```

◆ The whole list is enclosed in <OL> and </OL> or <UL> and </UL> tags.

◆ Each item in the list is enclosed in <LI> and </LI> tags.

Bullets

Bullets are normally round. You can set the style to SQUARE, DISK or ROUND with the TYPE option, like this:

<UL TYPE = DISK>

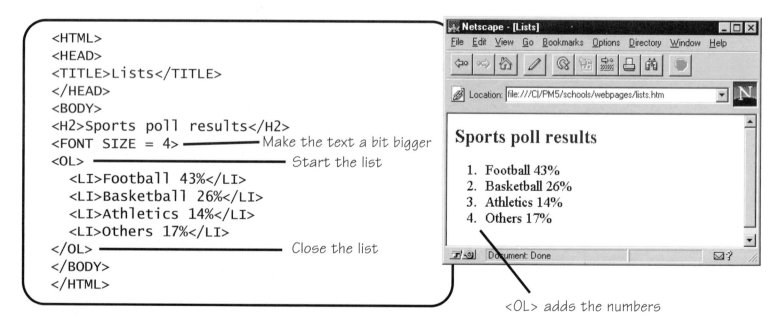

```
<HTML>
<HEAD>
<TITLE>Lists</TITLE>
</HEAD>
<BODY>
<H2>Sports poll results</H2>
<FONT SIZE = 4> ———————— Make the text a bit bigger
<OL> ———————————————— Start the list
  <LI>Football 43%</LI>
  <LI>Basketball 26%</LI>
  <LI>Athletics 14%</LI>
  <LI>Others 17%</LI>
</OL> ———————————— Close the list
</BODY>
</HTML>
```

Netscape - [Lists]

File Edit View Go Bookmarks Options Directory Window Help

Location: file:///C|/PM5/schools/webpages/lists.htm

Sports poll results

1. Football 43%
2. Basketball 26%
3. Athletics 14%
4. Others 17%

Document: Done

<OL> adds the numbers

Lines

<HR> (Horizontal Rule) draws lines. This is a single tag – there is no **</HR>**. A simple **<HR>** draws a thin line with a 3D effect. For variety, use the options:

SIZE to set the thickness. This is measured in pixels.

`<HR SIZE = 20>`   `Very thick line – almost a box`

WIDTH can be set in pixels, or as a percentage of the window width.

`<HR WIDTH = 400>`   `Fixed at 400 pixels wide`
`<HR WIDTH = 80%>`   `80% of the window's width`

NOSHADE makes the line solid.

`<HR SIZE = 10 NOSHADE>`   `Thick solid line`

With a percentage width the line adjusts to fit the window

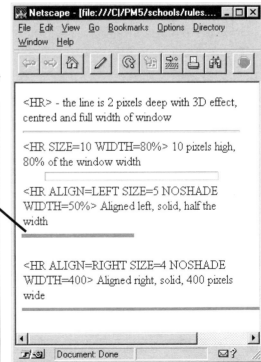

Netscape - [file:///C|/PM5/schools/rules.htm]

File   Edit   View   Go   Bookmarks   Options   Directory   Window   Help

<HR> - the line is 2 pixels deep with 3D effect, centred and full width of window

<HR SIZE=10 WIDTH=80%> 10 pixels high, 80% of the window width

<HR ALIGN=LEFT SIZE=5 NOSHADE WIDTH=50%> Aligned left, solid, half the width

<HR ALIGN=RIGHT SIZE=4 NOSHADE WIDTH=400> Aligned right, solid, 400 pixels wide

Document: Done

Netscape - [file:///C|/PM5/schools/rules....

File   Edit   View   Go   Bookmarks   Options   Directory   Window   Help

<HR> - the line is 2 pixels deep with 3D effect, centred and full width of window

<HR SIZE=10 WIDTH=80%> 10 pixels high, 80% of the window width

<HR ALIGN=LEFT SIZE=5 NOSHADE WIDTH=50%> Aligned left, solid, half the width

<HR ALIGN=RIGHT SIZE=4 NOSHADE WIDTH=400> Aligned right, solid, 400 pixels wide

Document: Done

Using images

Images make pages more attractive, but at a price. Image files are large compared to text files and even small images add to the downloading time. In the example opposite, the text takes 600 bytes – almost instant down-loading – while the picture is over 26Kb and takes around 10 seconds. So, include images, but keep your visitors happy by following these rules:

◆ Keep the images as small as possible;

◆ If you want to display large images – perhaps your own photo gallery, put them on separate (linked) pages and tell your visitors how big they will be.

◆ Include text describing the image, for the benefit of those who browse with AutoLoad Images turned off.

The basic image tag is:

```
<IMG SRC = "filename">
```

You can also use these options:

```
ALIGN = "left/center/right"
ALT = "description"
```

ALIGN sets the position of the image acros the page.

ALT is the text to display if the image is not loaded into a browser. In the example opposite, if image loading was turned off, you would see this:

A picture of me

Background images

You can 'tile' a page with the **BACKGROUND = "filename"** option in the <BODY> tag. The image is repeated across and down to fill the window.

Graphic formats

Images must be in GIF or JPG format for browsers to be able to display them. GIF files are usually smaller, but JPG s can use a larger set of colours. When you are preparing your images, try both formats and see which gives you the best size-to-quality balance.

If the images are in a different directory, you must give the path as well as the filename, e.g.

```
<IMG SRC="images/pic1.gif"
```

Make life easy for yourself – store your images in the same directory as the page files.

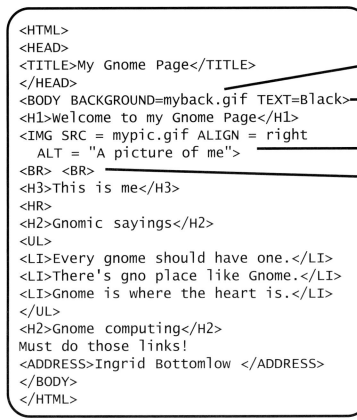

```
<HTML>
<HEAD>
<TITLE>My Gnome Page</TITLE>
</HEAD>
<BODY BACKGROUND=myback.gif TEXT=Black>
<H1>Welcome to my Gnome Page</H1>
<IMG SRC = mypic.gif ALIGN = right
  ALT = "A picture of me">
<BR> <BR>
<H3>This is me</H3>
<HR>
<H2>Gnomic sayings</H2>
<UL>
<LI>Every gnome should have one.</LI>
<LI>There's gno place like Gnome.</LI>
<LI>Gnome is where the heart is.</LI>
</UL>
<H2>Gnome computing</H2>
Must do those links!
<ADDRESS>Ingrid Bottomlow </ADDRESS>
</BODY>
</HTML>
```

Background image

Text colour Black

Image aligned to the right, with some ALT text

Two
s to force a larger space below text

The trick with background images is to use one which doesn't clash with the text. Very pale or bright images and black text work well. Here, the background image is the same as the main picture, but smaller and with fewer, paler colours – and if it was even simpler and paler, the text would be more readable.

93

Links

Links in a page

A link is created with a pair of tags. The first contains the URL of the page or file to be linked, and takes the form:

```
<A HREF=URL>
```

The second is a simple closing tag **</A>**.

The two enclose the image or text that becomes the clickable link, e.g.

```
<A HREF="http://www.yahoo.co.uk">Yahoo</A>
```

Yahoo will be displayed with an underline and in a different colour to the rest of the text. Clicking on it will take your visitor to Yahoo's UK site.

The link can be embedded within a larger item of text, e.g.

```
IT's Made Simple <A HREF="http://www.bh.com/
MadeSimple.htm"> here</A>
```

Only '**here**' is clickable in the *IT's Made Simple* line.

You can also use an image with, or instead of, text to make the link. Just place the **<A HREF...>** and **</A>** tags around the **<IMG SRC ...>** tag.

```
<A HREF="http://www.gnomeworld.gn"><IMG SRC =
"world.gif"></A>
```

You should include **ALT** text, or include text within the tags for the benefit of people who have the image loading turned off.

You can also add a link to give visitors an easy way to contact you. This line:

```
<A HREF = "mailto:me@my.e-mail.address"> Mail me </A>
```

opens a new mail message window, with your e-mail address in the **To:** slot.

If you have a page that runs over several screens, you might want to include links within the page, so that your readers can jump from one part to another.

Anchors

The clickable link follows the same pattern as above, but you must first define a named place, or **anchor**, to jump to.

```
<A NAME="Top">The start
of something big </A>
```

The anchor tags can fit round any text or image, and you can even leave it blank in between if you like.

The HREF tag is slightly different for a jump.

```
<A HREF = #Top> Return to
top of page </A>
```

Notice the # before the anchor name. This is essential.

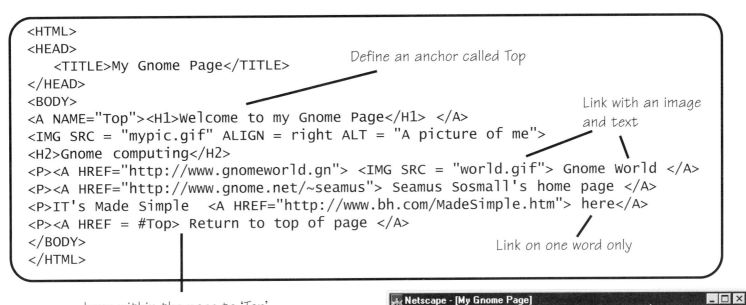

```
<HTML>
<HEAD>
    <TITLE>My Gnome Page</TITLE>
</HEAD>
<BODY>
<A NAME="Top"><H1>Welcome to my Gnome Page</H1> </A>
<IMG SRC = "mypic.gif" ALIGN = right ALT = "A picture of me">
<H2>Gnome computing</H2>
<P><A HREF="http://www.gnomeworld.gn"> <IMG SRC = "world.gif"> Gnome World </A>
<P><A HREF="http://www.gnome.net/~seamus"> Seamus Sosmall's home page </A>
<P>IT's Made Simple  <A HREF="http://www.bh.com/MadeSimple.htm"> here</A>
<P><A HREF = #Top> Return to top of page </A>
</BODY>
</HTML>
```

Define an anchor called Top

Link with an image and text

Link on one word only

Jump within the page to 'Top'

If you want to link to another page within your own site, all you need is the page name:

```
Meet <A HREF = "family.htm"> my family </A>
```

If the page is stored in a different directory, you will need to include the path – see page 97.

Linked images are outlined

Linked text is underlined

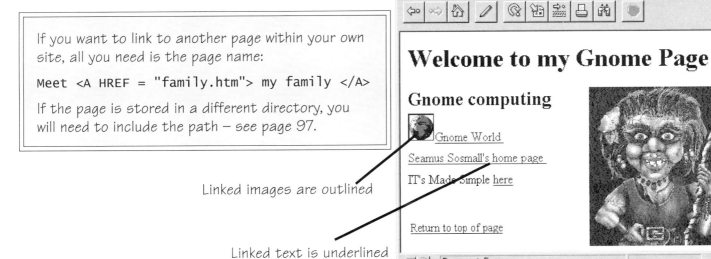

95

Organising the files

If you are creating a personal home page, file organisation is not a major problem – you just store all the pages, images and any other files in one directory. This simple approach won't work as well with a school Web site. If all the files were in one directory, there would be a danger of different people using the same filename and overwriting each others' files – it would also be very crowded!

The answer is to set up a structure of sub-directories. This should reflect the organisation of pages at the site.

> Start by creating the main pages – and the links between them. See how they look and test the links. If it's worth looking at – publish it . Other pages can be added later, as they are ready.

Suppose your site had this shape:

Top page with links to:

◆ admin and general information pages;

◆ what's new;

◆ pupils, main index, linking to...

　❖ year/group index pages, linking to...

　　◆ individual pupils' pages;

◆ links and resources;

　❖ subject/topic pages.

You should have a structure of directories within directories as shown here. Each directory at the lowest level belongs to one person, and will contain all of his or her files.

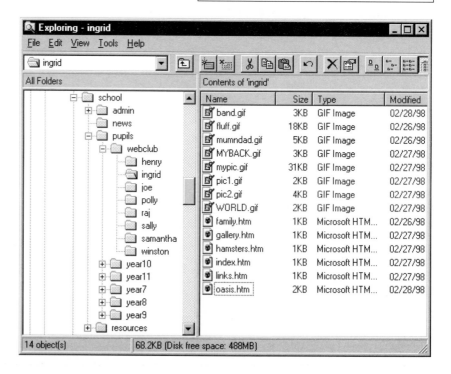

Links within a site

If you want to link to a file in another directory on your system, you must include the **path** to the file. This tells the computer where to look in the directory structure. If the directory is within the one containing the linking page, then you just give the directory name. With the directory structure shown in the example on page 96, a link from a page stored in the school directory to one in the admin sub-directory would look like this:

    <A HREF = "admin/main.htm">About the school</A>

To link to a page higher up, use .. (two dots), e.g.

    <A HREF = "../index.htm">Back to the top page</A>

Link to file in same directory

```
<HTML>
<HEAD>
<TITLE>Dotheboys Hall</TITLE>
</HEAD>
<BODY>
<H1 ALIGN = center>Dotheboys Hall</H1>
<H2 ALIGN = center>Welcome to our school</H2>
<BR><A HREF = "squires.htm">A message from Mr Squires</A>
<BR><A HREF = "admin/main.htm">About the school</A>
<BR><A HREF = "news/current.htm">Activities and events</A>
<BR><A HREF = "pupils/main.htm">Pupils' pages</A>
<BR><A HREF = "resources/index.htm">Links and other resources</A>
</BODY>
</HTML>
```

Link to file in sub-directory

Netscape - [Dotheboys Hall]

File Edit View Go Bookmarks Options Directory Window Help

Location: Files/Microsoft FrontPage/web/school/index.htm

Dotheboys Hall

Welcome to our school

A message from Mr Squires
About the school
Activities and events
Pupils' pages
Links and other resources

Document: Done

Tables and layout

Don't miss out on tables! Don't think that tables are just for setting out loads of boring figures. (Though you can use them for that as well!) Tables are the key to good layouts. They let you arrange images and text in rows and columns of varying sizes, giving you magazine-style layouts on screen.

Be warned, they are fiddly to create – though a good HTML editor (see page 104) will make it much easier.

A table is marked by the tags **<TABLE>** and **</TABLE>**. The first tag can take options. The most important of these is **BORDER**, which sets the thickness of the border, in pixels. Other options control the spacing between the cells, the colour and a few other things.

Each row in the table must be enclosed in the tags **<TR>** and **</TR>**.

Each cell within a row must be enclosed in the tags **<TD>** and **</TD>**.

Here's about the simplest table you could create:

```
<TABLE BORDER=1 >
<TR>
<TD>Left cell </TD>
<TD>Right cell </TD>
</TR>
</TABLE>
```

And that looks like this:

Left cell	Right cell

<TABLE> options

CELLSPACING sets the distance between the cells, e.g.

```
CELLSPACING =4
```

CELLPADDING sets the distance between the edge of a cells and the text or image in it, e.g.

```
CELLPADDING = 2
```

WIDTH and **HEIGHT** can be set in pixels or as a percentage of the window – as in the **<IMG SRC>** tag, e.g.

```
WIDTH = 75%
```
or
```
WIDTH = 200 HEIGHT  = 100
```

BGCOLOR sets the colour of the background of the whole table, e.g.

```
BGCOLOR =Yellow
```

<TR> and <TD> options

WIDTH, HEIGHT and BGCOLOR can be set for a row in the <TR> tag, or for an individual cell in the <TD> tag. The ALIGN option can also be used here to align text within a cell..

```
<HTML>
<HEAD>
    <TITLE>My Gnome Page</TITLE>
</HEAD>
<H2>Scenes from the Dribble Valley</H2>
<CENTER>
<TABLE BORDER=8 CELLSPACING=8 CELLPADDING=4 WIDTH=90% BGCOLOR=Yellow >
<TR>
  <TD><IMG SRC="bar.gif"></TD>
  <TD>The Green Gnome. If you drink the scrumpy,that's the colour you go.</TD>
</TR>
<TR>
  <TD>The Dribblemouth light.500 glow-worms power its mighty beam.</TD>
<TD><IMG SRC="light.gif"></TD>
</TR>
</TABLE>
</CENTER>
</BODY>
</HTML>
```

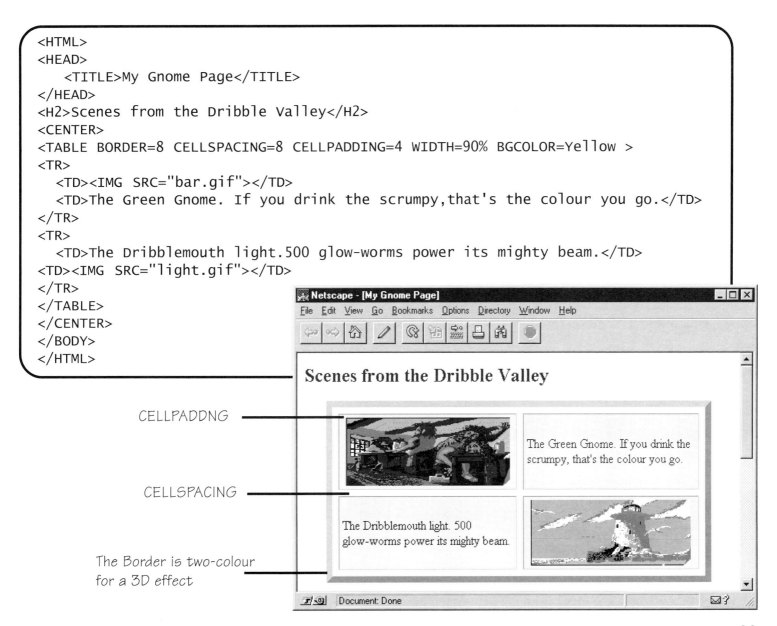

CELLPADDNG

CELLSPACING

The Border is two-colour
for a 3D effect

99

Tables without borders

Thick borders and coloured backgrounds can make tables into attractive features. The effect can be made even more striking by picking out rows or individual cells in different colours and using coloured text.

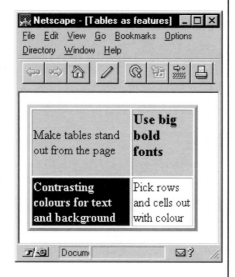

Approach them from the other way, setting BORDER = 0 and with the background colour the same as the page, and the table disappears – leaving just the layout. This can also be a good thing.

You can make one cell span across several columns by using the **COLSPAN** option in its **<TD>** tag. The heading in the example was produced by this:

```
<TD COLSPAN = 2>
<H1>Tables without borders </H1>
</TD>
```

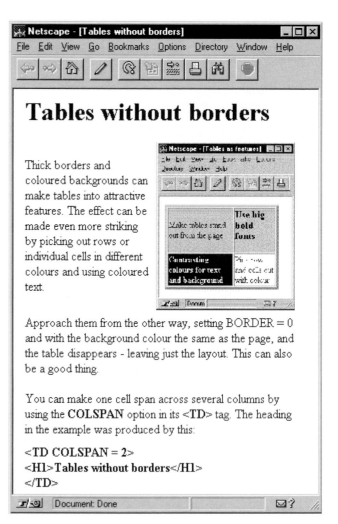

With tables, you can create pages that look just like pages in books! Experiment.

Forms and feedback

Would you like visitors to your Web site to be able to get touch with you? The simplest way to do this is to include a **mailto:** link (see page 101), so that they can drop you an e-mail. The better way is to use a **form**. Visitors can enter data into a form, and the data is then sent to you.

A form starts with the **<FORM>** tag. This has two options:

METHOD = defines how the form data is to be handled, and is usually **Post**;

ACTION = tells the visitor's browser what to do next. The simplest is a **mailto:** link, which makes the browser mail the form's data directly to you.

The top line of a form should be something like this:

```
<FORM METHOD=Post ACTION=mailto:name@address>
```

And the last line must be a closing tag **</FORM>**.

All data is collected in **<INPUT...>** tags. In their simplest form these create on-line text boxes, e.g.

```
<INPUT NAME = visitor>
<INPUT NAME = address>
```

The first creates a text box called 'visitor'; the second is called 'address'. The NAME is essential to identify the data. When the form's data is sent to you, it will include the phrases 'visitor = Joe Bloggs' (or whoever sent it) and 'address = jbloggs@worldnet.co.uk'.

```
<INPUT TYPE = submit VALUE = "Send">
```

This creates a clickable button labelled "Send". When this is clicked, the ACTION is carried out – sending the data to you.

You can see these in action in the next example.

Forms can contain:

◆ one-line and multi-line text boxes, where visitors can enter text;

◆ radio buttons, checkboxes and menus, where visitors can make choices;

◆ command buttons to send the data or clear the form.

CGI scripts

Unfortunately, ACTION=mailto: only works if your visitors are using a Netscape browser. The better way is to use a special CGI script (small program) on your service provider's computer. These vary. Ask you service provider about CGI scripts for form feedback.

101

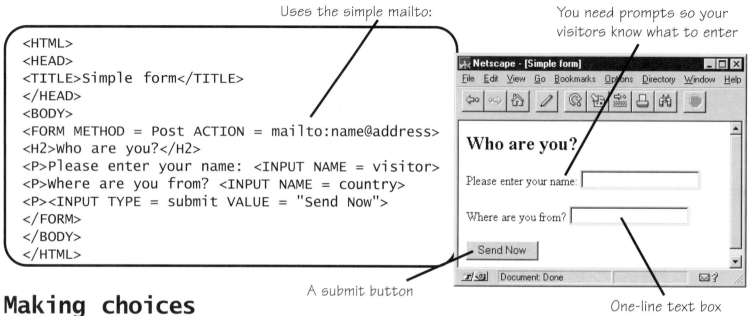

Uses the simple mailto:

You need prompts so your visitors know what to enter

```
<HTML>
<HEAD>
<TITLE>Simple form</TITLE>
</HEAD>
<BODY>
<FORM METHOD = Post ACTION = mailto:name@address>
<H2>Who are you?</H2>
<P>Please enter your name: <INPUT NAME = visitor>
<P>Where are you from? <INPUT NAME = country>
<P><INPUT TYPE = submit VALUE = "Send Now">
</FORM>
</BODY>
</HTML>
```

A submit button

One-line text box

Making choices

Checkboxes and radio buttons are useful for collecting organised data – perhaps for a survey. Checkboxes produce **on** or **off** results.

```
<P>Do you use the canteen:
<BR><INPUT TYPE = checkbox NAME = break> At break
```

If the user puts a tick in the break checkbox, when the form is returned it will have the phrase 'break = on'.

Radio buttons are always used in sets, and only one of these can be on. Notice that the NAME is the same for all the buttons in the set.

```
<P>What do you normally do for lunch?
<BR><INPUT TYPE = radio NAME = meal>School meal
<BR><INPUT TYPE = radio NAME = meal>Packed lunch
<BR><INPUT TYPE = radio NAME = meal>Go home
```

Reset buttons

If you want to give your visitors a chance to rub out their answers and start again, add a **reset** button. This clears the text boxes and resets the checkboxes and radio buttons to their original state.

```
<INPUT TYPE = reset VALUE
= "Clear and restart">
```

```
<HTML>
<HEAD>
<TITLE>Forms for feedback</TITLE>
</HEAD>
<BODY>
<FORM METHOD = Post ACTION = mailto:name@address>
<H2>School canteen survey</H2>
<P>Your name: <INPUT NAME = visitor>
<P>Do you use the canteen:
<BR><INPUT TYPE = checkbox NAME = break> At break
<BR><INPUT TYPE = checkbox NAME = lunch> At lunch

<P>What do you normally do for lunch?
<BR><INPUT TYPE = radio NAME = meal>School meal
<BR><INPUT TYPE = radio NAME = meal>Packed lunch
<BR><INPUT TYPE = radio NAME = meal>Go home

<P><INPUT TYPE = submit VALUE = "Submit results">
<INPUT TYPE = reset VALUE = "Clear and restart">

</FORM>
</BODY>
</HTML>
```

Use radio buttons where you want your visitor to select one from a set; checkboxes where the visitor can select any or all of them.

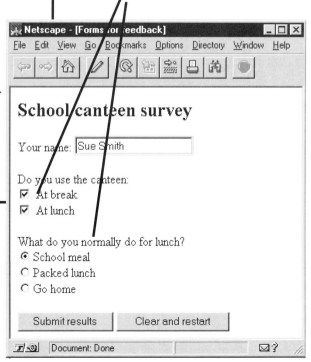

Forms can also contain drop-down menus and multi-line text boxes. If you want to know more about these – or other aspects of HTML, try *HTML Made Simple* from Butterworth-Heinemann.

Netscape's Editor

The editor in Netscape Gold (called Composer in the new Netscape Communicator pacakge) is easy to use and handles most aspects of HTML. It has no tools for creating forms, or for building frames (sub-divided windows) – areas where many HTML editors also struggle. However, it is very good for handling text, images, links and tables. It also provides an easy way to upload files to your service provider when you are ready to publish your home page.

> If you want to fine-tune the HTML, or add tags that the editor cannot handle, you can take the code into your word processor and work on it there.

The editor window

Use the editor as you would any word processor.

To set font size, emphasis or colour, first select the text then click a button on the **Character Format toolbar**.

Style (Heading 1, Address, etc.), alignment and indents can only be applied to whole paragraphs. These are set from the **Paragraph Format toolbar**.

To insert an anchor, images, lines or tables, place the cursor where you want it to go, then click the appropriate button. A **Properties** dialog box will open to get the details of the image, the size of the table and other details. If you want to change any of these later, right click on the object to get the shortcut menu and select **Properties** to reopen the dialog box.

This makes it a bit easier to define images and lines, but far, far easier to create tables than writing the HTML code yourself!

> The hardest part of creating a page can be deciding what goes on it; the next hardest is planning the layout. The templates and wizards at Netscape's home page can help with this. Use your browser to go to:
>
> http://www.netscape.com

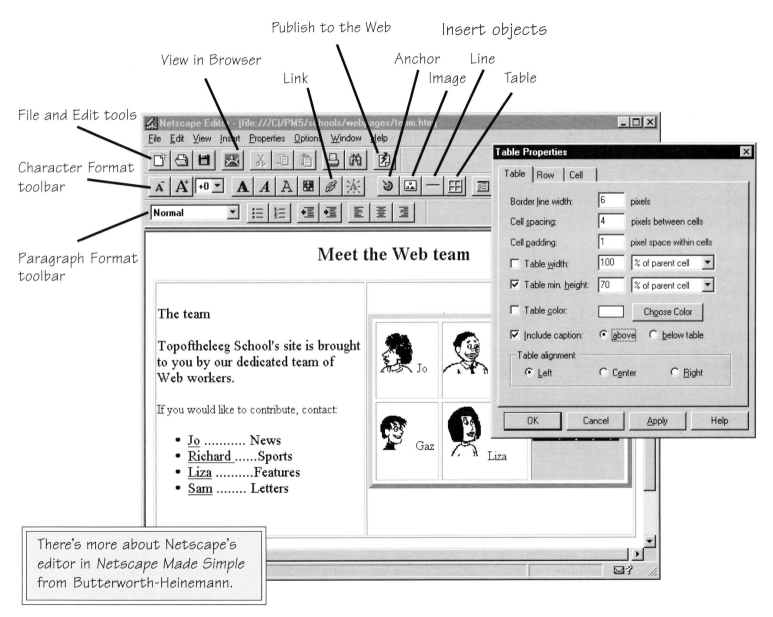

Publish to the Web

Insert objects

View in Browser

Anchor   Line

Link   Image   Table

File and Edit tools

Character Format toolbar

Paragraph Format toolbar

Netscape Editor - [file:///C|/PM5/schools/webpages/team.htm]

File   Edit   View   Insert   Properties   Options   Window   Help

Normal

Meet the Web team

The team

Topoftheleeg School's site is brought to you by our dedicated team of Web workers.

If you would like to contribute, contact:

- <u>Jo</u> .... News
- <u>Richard</u> ......Sports
- <u>Liza</u> ....Features
- <u>Sam</u> .... Letters

Jo

Gaz

Liza

Table Properties

Table | Row | Cell

Border line width: 6   pixels

Cell spacing: 4   pixels between cells

Cell padding: 1   pixel space within cells

☐ Table width: 100   % of parent cell

☑ Table min. height: 70   % of parent cell

☐ Table color: Choose Color

☑ Include caption: ⊙ above   ○ below table

Table alignment
  ⊙ Left   ○ Center   ○ Right

OK   Cancel   Apply   Help

There's more about Netscape's editor in *Netscape Made Simple* from Butterworth-Heinemann.

105

FrontPage

FrontPage is more than just an HTML editor. It is a complete Web site management system. It does have an editor – and a very good one too. This can do everything that the Netscape Editor can do, and more besides.

Among the more useful extras are its collections of backgrounds, dividing lines, animations and other images. These offer a quick and easy way to brighten up a page.

Other features of the editor include:

◆ better table formatting – more flexible cell layouts, multi-coloured borders and background images;

◆ choice of fonts (though these may be replaced by standard fonts in visitors' browsers);

◆ simpler form construction and routines to get feedback;

◆ background sounds;

◆ marquees – scrolling, decorated text (though these can only be seen by Internet Explorer users);

◆ you can have several pages open at the same time – useful when you are linking them, or copying features from one to another.

> Internet Explorer 4.0 includes FrontPage Express, a slightly cut-down version of the FrontPage editor.

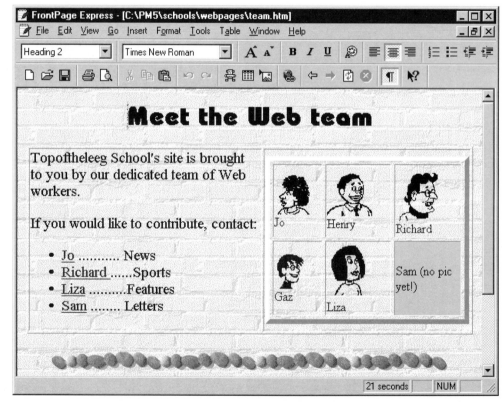

Web site management

School Web sites need managing! Even a small site will have contributions from several different people, be split over several directories, and have some of its pages changed fairly regularly. Someone will have to keep an eye on it to make sure that files are in the right place and that the links between the pages are correct – especially after updating. This can be done 'by hand', but is much simpler with site management software like FrontPage.

When a page is selected from the All Hyperlinks panel on the left, it becomes the centre of the display on the right. You can then see which pages are linked from it – and to it.

FrontPage's Explorer shows the links between pages and the organisation of files. Its tools give you control over the site.

◆ files can be deleted or moved;

◆ links (both within and beyond the site) can be checked and edited;

◆ all the files in the site, or just those that have been edited recently can be uploaded to your service provider.

If you want to know more, try FrontPage Made Simple from Butterworth-Heinemann.

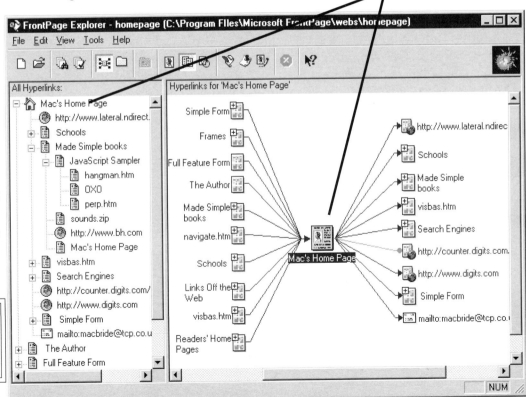

107

Things To Do

1 Create a Favourite Places page containing links to those sites that you find most interesting, useful or fun to visit. The links should be organised into categories.

2 Text-only pages are quick to download and need not be boring. Experiment with colour and different size fonts to see what you can do, using only text.

3 Animated GIFs can add life to a page. Use a search engine to find out what they are and how they are created. Ready-made GIFs can be found on the Internet, but if you want to create your own you need suitable software. (Try Microsoft GIF Animator – it's part of the FrontPage package and may be available from their site at **http://www.microsoft.com**. If you cannot find it there, try The Software Library at **http://www.hotfiles.com**.)

If you come across a great Web page and want to know how it was created, use the View Document Source command to see the HTML code.

For closer study of a page, use File Save As to save it on your hard disk. You can then open it in an HTML editor or word-processor and examine or experiment with it.

You must not simply copy someone else's page and publish it as your own. All Web pages are the copyright of their authors, even if they have not included a © line.

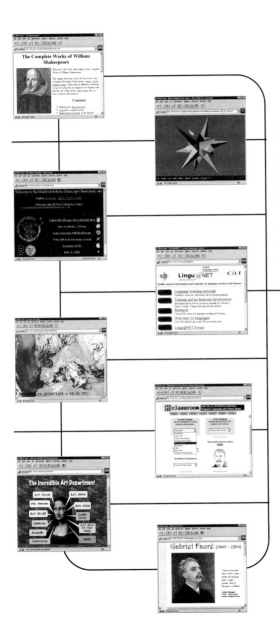

7 Curriculum areas

For some subjects there are sites packed with ideas and links, specifically geared towards UK schools. For other subjects, you have to look harder to find relevant resources or good starting places. This chapter aims to point you towards some useful sites, or at least to give you an idea of what you can find.

English

The Internet reading room

For some time, academics and enthusiasts around the world have putting literature on-line, so that now a great store can be read through the Web. There may be fewer books here than in your local library, but not necessarily the same ones – you won't find Dick Francis but you will find Francis Bacon.

Many newspapers and magazines have Web sites (see page 58), and new 'e-zines' (electronic magazines) keep appearing. All can be good sources of information and inspiration.

Dictionaries, thesauruses and other reference books are on-line – you will find Webster's here, and the Oxford dictionary (though they charge).

On-line books have some advantages:

◆ Any number of people can read the same book at once.

◆ Quotes can be copied from the text and pasted into an essay in a word-processor.

◆ Some on-line books have linked notes, which can be read if needed or ignored if the reader does not want to break the flow of the text.

Read Shakespeare on-line at:
http://the-tech.mit.edu/Shakespeare/works.html

The On-Line Books Page

This has the fullest listing of the books available on-line. Go to:

http://www.cs.cmu.edu/
bookauthors.html

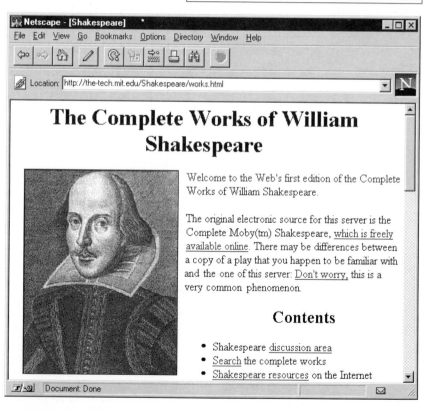

The Complete Works of William Shakespeare

Welcome to the Web's first edition of the Complete Works of William Shakespeare.

The original electronic source for this server is the Complete Moby(tm) Shakespeare, which is freely available online. There may be differences between a copy of a play that you happen to be familiar with and the one of this server: Don't worry, this is a very common phenomenon.

Contents

• Shakespeare discussion area
• Search the complete works
• Shakespeare resources on the Internet

Publishing pupils' work

If you have set up your own Web site, you can publish work by pupils on its pages. It takes very little effort to convert a word-processed file into hypertext – most newer word-processors offer HTML as a format to save files. Once on the Web, it will have – potentially – an international audience, though the real readers are more likely to be other pupils or family members linking in from their homes.

If you really want work to reach a wider audience, there are a number of Web magazines that specialise in publishing work by young people. One of the best established of these is KidPub, US-based but with contributors and readers from all over the world.

Schools that subscribe to CampusWorld can send material in to its Swift magazine.

KidPub is worth a visit even if you don't intend publishing there.
Find it at:

http://www.kidpub.org/kidpub/

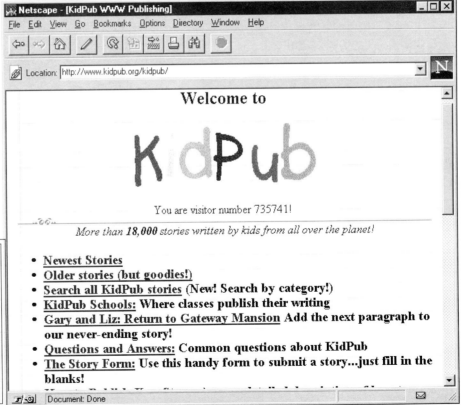

English Teaching in the UK

This is a great site, created by Harry Dodds (Head of English at Gosford Hill School). For links, ideas and more, visit:

http://www.gosford-hill.oxon.sch.uk/
etuk/etuk.htm

Maths

There is an amazing amount of maths-related material on the Internet, in a vast number of sites – probably because there have been a lot of mathematicians among the Internet enthusiasts since its early days.

There are investigations, tutorials, demonstrations across the whole range mathematics and for all levels, plus puzzles and games, which can be a great source of stimulus.

There are also plenty of sites where data can be found for use in statistics, graphing and other data-handling projects, or you can collect your own data through e-mail surveys. (See *Classroom connections*, page 140).

One of the best places to start your exploring is **MathsNet**. It has lots of material within its site, and excellent links to the wider Web.

MathsNet is at:

http://www.anglia.co.uk/education/ mathsnet

MathsNet is a great site – it even has a Floating Calculator that you can keep on screen while you work at the site!

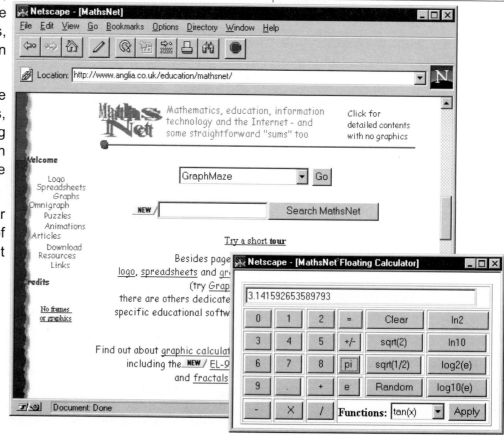

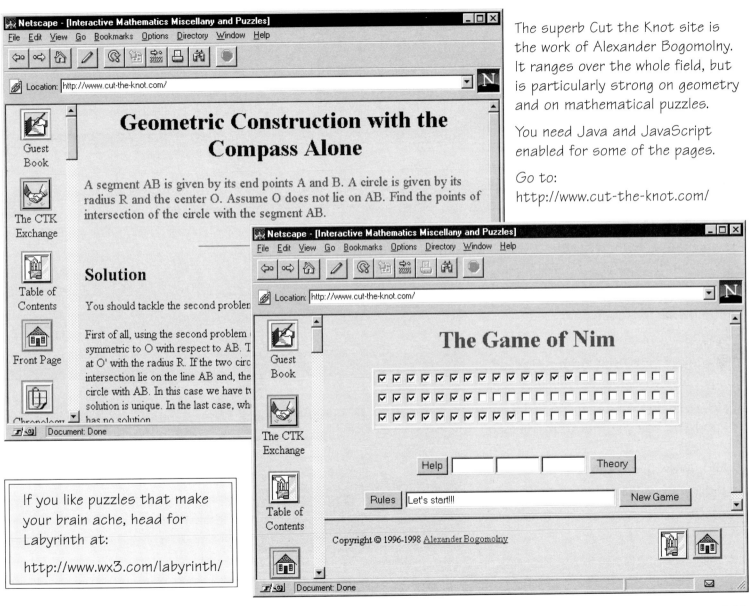

The superb Cut the Knot site is the work of Alexander Bogomolny. It ranges over the whole field, but is particularly strong on geometry and on mathematical puzzles.

You need Java and JavaScript enabled for some of the pages.

Go to:
http://www.cut-the-knot.com/

If you like puzzles that make your brain ache, head for Labyrinth at:

http://www.wx3.com/labyrinth/

Geometric Construction with the Compass Alone

A segment AB is given by its end points A and B. A circle is given by its radius R and the center O. Assume O does not lie on AB. Find the points of intersection of the circle with the segment AB.

Solution

You should tackle the second problem

First of all, using the second problem symmetric to O with respect to AB. T at O' with the radius R. If the two circ intersection lie on the line AB and, the circle with AB. In this case we have tw solution is unique. In the last case, wh has no solution.

The Game of Nim

Copyright © 1996-1998 Alexander Bogomolny

Virtual Polyhedra

If you are into 3D geometry, this is the place to go – though you may need to do some work on your browser first. The polyhedra are displayed using VRML (Virtual Reality Modelling Language), which lets you move around the model – it's almost as good as having a real solid model!

Browsers need help to handle VRML.

Netscape 3.0 needs the Live3D plug-in. Go to Netscape's home site at:

http://www.netscape.com/

and search for Live3D.

The equivalent for Communicator is Cosmo, also available at Netscape.

Internet Explorer 4.0 needs the VRML add-on, and you can get that from Microsoft. Head for:

http://www.microsoft.com/ie/download

and follow the links to the add-ons.

'Virtual Polyhedra' is being created by George W. Hart of Hofstra University. Find it at:

http://www.li.net/~george/virtual-polyhedra/vp.html

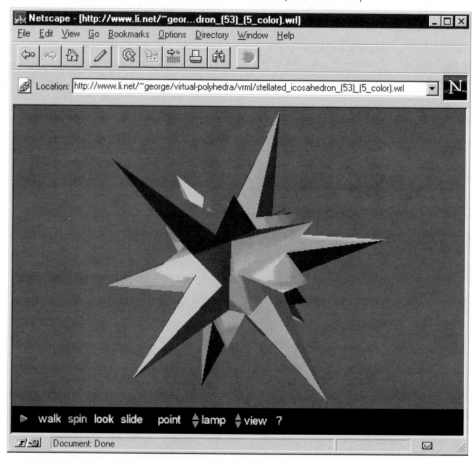

Science

Scientists have been closely involved in the development of the Internet from the start – the World Wide Web was devised by a scientist at CERN (the European research centre) – and scientists in education have been quick off the mark in producing Web resources.

One of the best starting points for Science is probably the Schools Online Science site at: **http://www.shu.ac.uk/schools/sci/sol/contents.htm**. It has a Library of links (see the next page); a Cafe where you can swap ideas and information with other people in schools, and ask the experts; a Lab with resources for experiments – joint projects can be arranged here; and a Prep room for staff.

Science on the Internet is not just about reading and exchanging information. Two examples of other ways in which the Internet can be valuable in Science are illustrated on the next two pages.

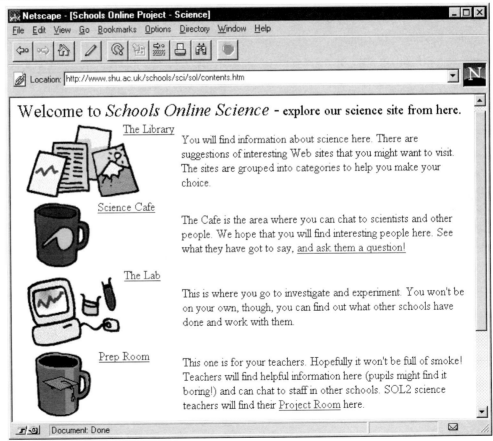

Netscape - [Schools Online Project - Science]

File Edit View Go Bookmarks Options Directory Window Help

Location: http://www.shu.ac.uk/schools/sci/sol/contents.htm

Welcome to *Schools Online Science* - explore our science site from here.

The Library

You will find information about science here. There are suggestions of interesting Web sites that you might want to visit. The sites are grouped into categories to help you make your choice.

Science Cafe

The Cafe is the area where you can chat to scientists and other people. We hope that you will find interesting people here. See what they have got to say, and ask them a question!

The Lab

This is where you go to investigate and experiment. You won't be on your own, though, you can find out what other schools have done and work with them.

Prep Room

This one is for your teachers. Hopefully it won't be full of smoke! Teachers will find helpful information here (pupils might find it boring!) and can chat to staff in other schools. SOL2 science teachers will find their Project Room here.

Document: Done

The Library

At the Schools Online Science Library, the links are grouped into categories. Browsing through these can be a good way to get an idea of the range of resources that are available online.

If you are looking for information on a topic, try the Search, but don't expect too much. It only searches through the limited information held within the Library. Given a fairly general topic, it will point you to the relevant categories. If you are looking for something very specific, you would probably do better at one of the Internet's search engines, such as Infoseek (page 44).

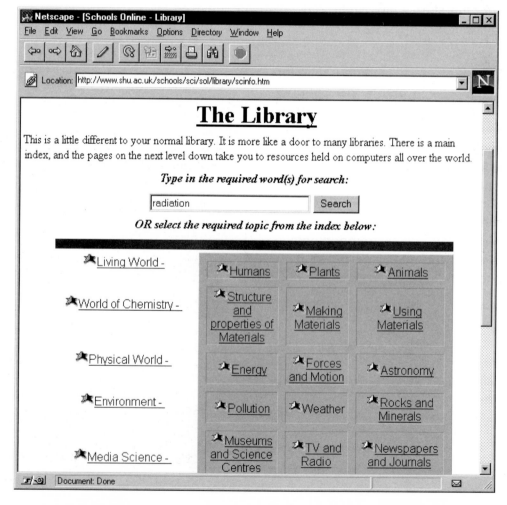

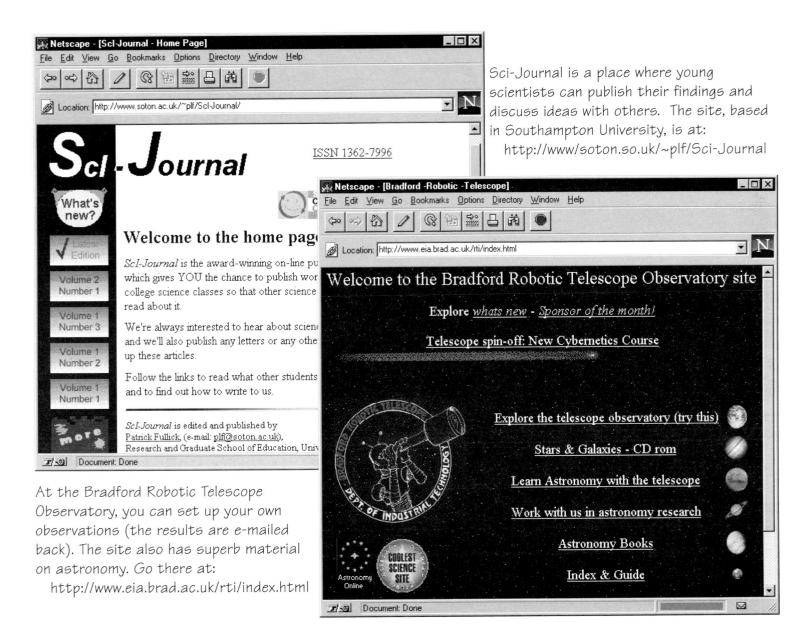

Sci-Journal is a place where young scientists can publish their findings and discuss ideas with others. The site, based in Southampton University, is at:

http://www/soton.so.uk/~plf/Sci-Journal

At the Bradford Robotic Telescope Observatory, you can set up your own observations (the results are e-mailed back). The site also has superb material on astronomy. Go there at:

http://www.eia.brad.ac.uk/rti/index.html

Modern Languages

E-mail links

One of the most exciting ways to use the Internet for Modern Languages is to set up an e-mail link with native speakers of the target language. Well-organised e-mail links can add immediacy and impact to learning, but they must be properly planned.

Aims

Is the aim to find out about life in the target country, or to build reading and/or writing skills in the language?

English or the foreign language?

Which language should you communicate in? This will depend on the age and ability of the students, and the wishes of the partner school. A carefully structured mix may be the answer.

Timescale

Unless you have an existing (non-e-mail) relationship with the school and its students, it may be difficult to keep the e-mail link going for long. A time-limited link – preferably anchored around the exchange of specific information – is more likely to succeed. Any long-term links that grow out of this could be a bonus.

Content

A simple exchange of personal information is not going to get anyone very far. There must be a core topic to give focus and impetus to the link.

Web resources

There's plenty of stimulus material and reading matter on the Web – the problem, as always, is sorting the wheat from the chaff. Rather than do this all yourself, you may prefer to start at Lingu@NET or the Schools Online project.

Both offer good sets of selected links, as well as sensible advice on the use of the Internet in modern languages and a place to discuss ideas with other teachers and students.

The **Schools Online project** has an excellent Modern Languages centre. Its main site is at:

> http://sol.ultralab.anglia.ac.uk/

From the top page, follow the links to **Schools Online**, then **Modern Languages**.

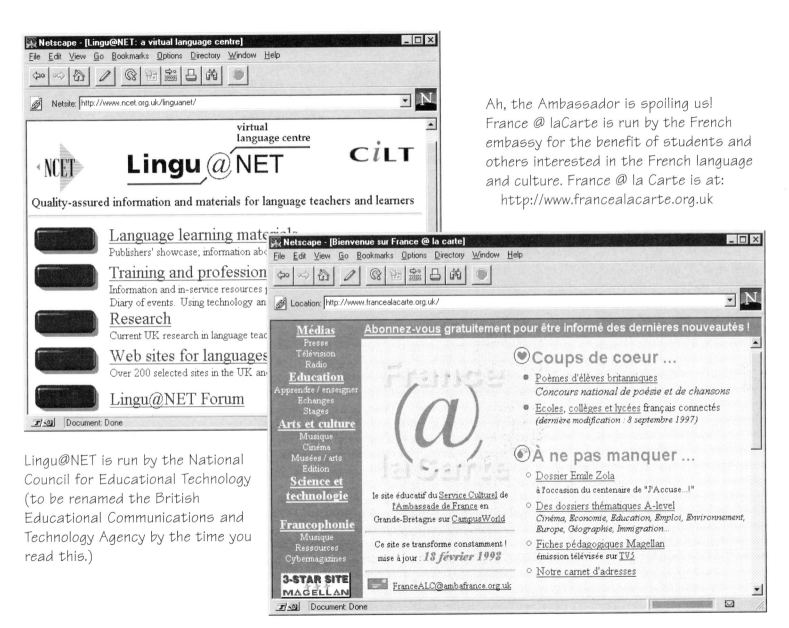

Ah, the Ambassador is spoiling us! France @ laCarte is run by the French embassy for the benefit of students and others interested in the French language and culture. France @ la Carte is at: http://www.francealacarte.org.uk

Lingu@NET is run by the National Council for Educational Technology (to be renamed the British Educational Communications and Technology Agency by the time you read this.)

119

Geography

The Internet has given geographers faster and easier access to information from all over the world, than ever before.

Weather images

Satellite and radar images are readily available – often within minutes of being taken. This image in this example was 6 hours old by the time I got it, but I guess I was a little slow! This came from Meteo France, via WeatherImages at:

http://www.weatherimages.org/

On-line cooperation

A more active use of the Internet is to set up e-mail links with schools overseas and exchange weather and other local data. (See *Classroom connections*, page 140.)

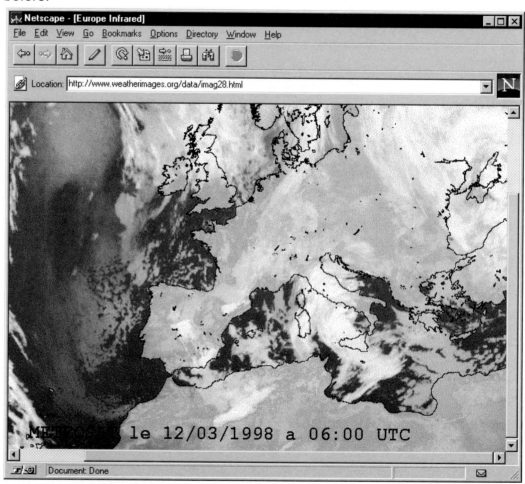

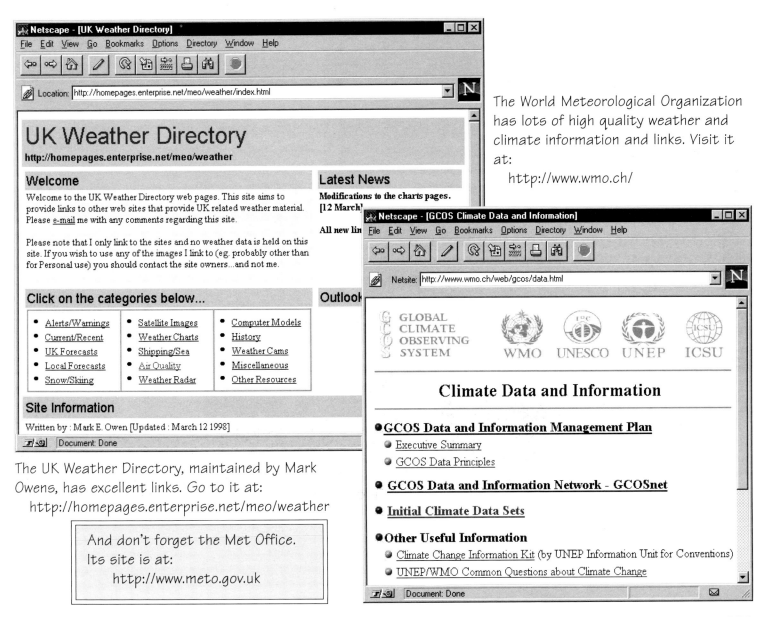

The World Meteorological Organization has lots of high quality weather and climate information and links. Visit it at:

http://www.wmo.ch/

The UK Weather Directory, maintained by Mark Owens, has excellent links. Go to it at:

http://homepages.enterprise.net/meo/weather

And don't forget the Met Office. Its site is at:

http://www.meto.gov.uk

121

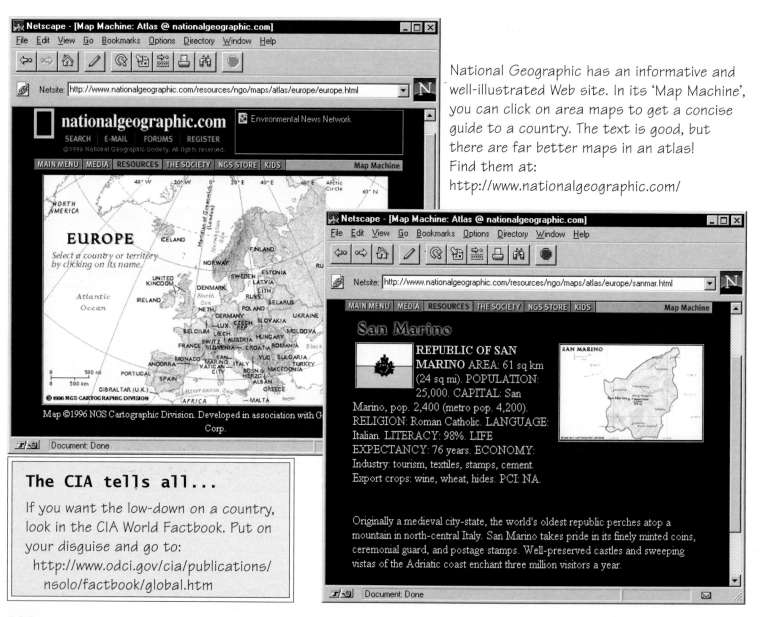

National Geographic has an informative and well-illustrated Web site. In its 'Map Machine', you can click on area maps to get a concise guide to a country. The text is good, but there are far better maps in an atlas!
Find them at:
http://www.nationalgeographic.com/

The CIA tells all...

If you want the low-down on a country, look in the CIA World Factbook. Put on your disguise and go to:
http://www.odci.gov/cia/publications/ nsolo/factbook/global.htm

History

There are masses of resources for schools' History on the Internet, but no ideal starting point. Yahoo has thousands of links on its History menu – reach it through Arts, then Humanities. They are well-organised, with links grouped either by century or by topic, but they are not directly related to the UK school curriculum.

One site that is very much rooted in the curriculum is Sky's History Channel. It has links and articles from History Review written for A level and GCSE students (and information about Sky's broadcasts). Go to:

http://www.sky.co.uk/history/classroom/

Another UK site that may be worth a visit is Britannia Magazine. Amongst other features, they have a Timeline of British history, with concise summaries of key events and people. They are at:

http://www.britannia.com

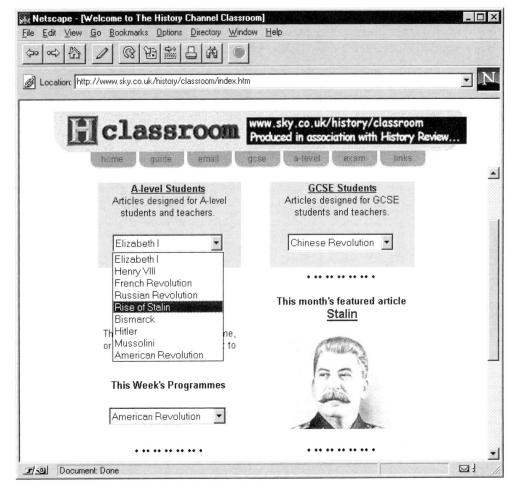

Historical documents

This copy of the newspaper report of Parliament's decision to execute King Charles I is an example of some of the historical documents that can be read on the Internet. (It looks better printed, preferably on slightly crinkled yellowing paper.)

Though the language may be hard, the spelling odd and the typeface difficult to read, working from the original documents really drives home the message that today's news is tomorrow's history.

The Intelligencer is just one of the papers to be found at:

http://members.aa.net/~davidco/ History/

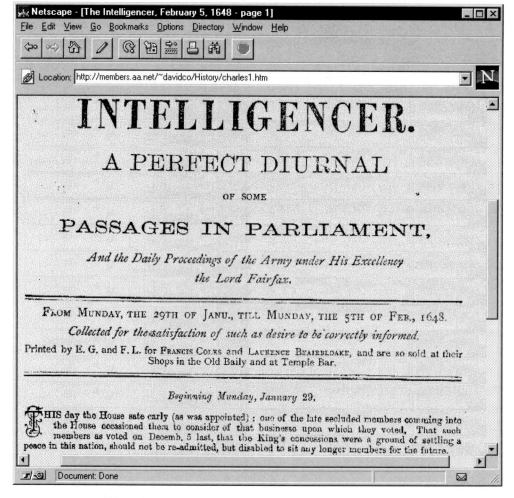

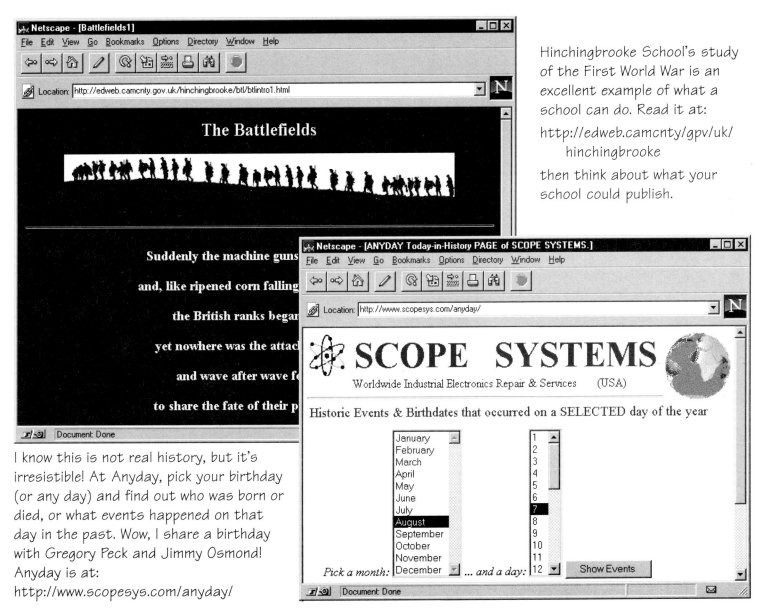

Hinchingbrooke School's study of the First World War is an excellent example of what a school can do. Read it at:

http://edweb.camcnty/gpv/uk/
    hinchingbrooke

then think about what your school could publish.

I know this is not real history, but it's irresistible! At Anyday, pick your birthday (or any day) and find out who was born or died, or what events happened on that day in the past. Wow, I share a birthday with Gregory Peck and Jimmy Osmond! Anyday is at:
http://www.scopesys.com/anyday/

125

Art

The best jumping off point into the Web for visual and other arts is World Wide Arts Resources (**http://wwar.com**). This has links to several thousand selected sites and searchable databases of artists, museums, galleries, dance and other resources.

Less comprehensive, but perhaps more fun, is the Incredible Art Department at **http://www.artswire.org/kenroar/**. (You can't see it in this still screenshot, but the Mona Lisa is animated!) This is school-centred, and a good source of stimulus.

If you are creating a school Web site, why not include an Art Gallery to display pupils' work? Pictures can be scanned in, or captured with a digital camera, and – don't forget – you can create art directly on the computer with graphics software.

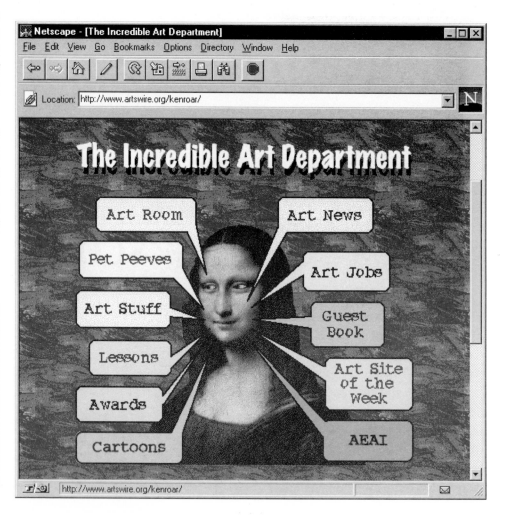

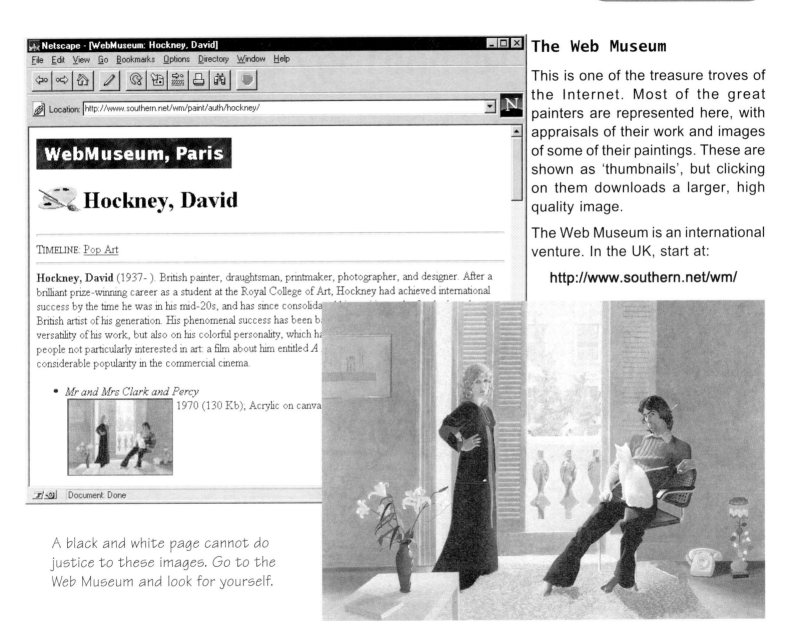

Netscape - [WebMuseum: Hockney, David]

File Edit View Go Bookmarks Options Directory Window Help

Location: http://www.southern.net/wm/paint/auth/hockney/

WebMuseum, Paris

Hockney, David

TIMELINE: Pop Art

Hockney, David (1937-). British painter, draughtsman, printmaker, photographer, and designer. After a brilliant prize-winning career as a student at the Royal College of Art, Hockney had achieved international success by the time he was in his mid-20s, and has since consolida[...] British artist of his generation. His phenomenal success has been b[...] versatility of his work, but also on his colorful personality, which ha[...] people not particularly interested in art: a film about him entitled *A* [...] considerable popularity in the commercial cinema.

- *Mr and Mrs Clark and Percy*
  1970 (130 Kb); Acrylic on canva[...]

Document: Done

The Web Museum

This is one of the treasure troves of the Internet. Most of the great painters are represented here, with appraisals of their work and images of some of their paintings. These are shown as 'thumbnails', but clicking on them downloads a larger, high quality image.

The Web Museum is an international venture. In the UK, start at:

http://www.southern.net/wm/

A black and white page cannot do justice to these images. Go to the Web Museum and look for yourself.

Design and Technology

The Internet is, of course, packed with technology, though not necessarily of the type that is wanted in schools. There's also plenty of design – but a search for this will find mainly 'Web designers'.

Designercity is a site celebrating British designers and inventors. The emphasis is on the fashion industry, but there is a good section on architecture and a fascinating account of the work of Sir Clive Sinclair – he had a long history of successful innovation before getting stuck in the electric car traffic jam.

Explore the best of British design at:
http:www.designer.com/

Fashion Net is another good starting point for finding links to fashion pages.

Find it at:

http://www.fashion.net

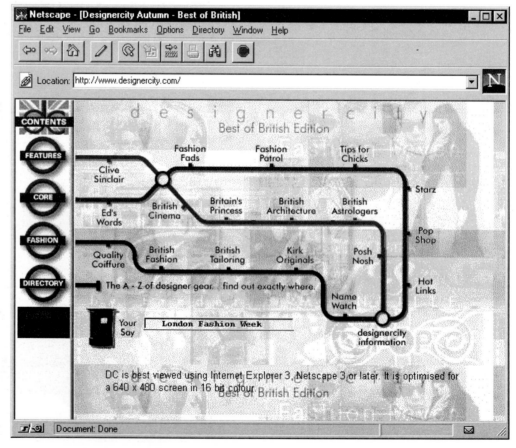

Music

At the time of writing, there seems to be very little on the Internet which is directly related to music as a UK curriculum subject. There are, however, lots of music resources.

The best collection of selected music links is at the Worldwide Internet Music Resources site in the Indiana University School of Music. Its URL is:

> http://www.music.indiana.edu/
> music_resources/

Amongst other things it has links to every composer I've heard of, and dozens that I haven't.

For links to performance music – youth and professional, and other UK music resources, try OrchestraNet at:

> http://www.orchestranet.co.uk/

The Web is great for researching instruments – history, construction, music, artists. Yahoo has an Instruments menu in its Music section, or run a search at Infoseek.

Beautifully presented, and well-written, the Fauré page by Susan Martin is a good example of the biographies that can be reached from the Indiana School of Music.

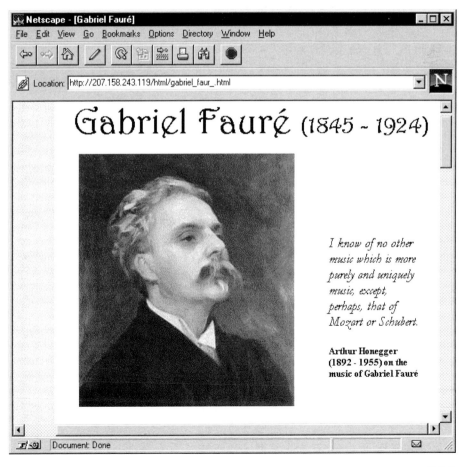

Physical Education

Many sporting bodies in the UK and elsewhere have been making good use of the Internet for some time, as it is an ideal way to communicate with players, organisers and fans who may be spread over a wide area. As a result of this, the sports aspect of the PE curriculum is very well covered.

The School Page UK is at:
http://www.eyesoftime.com/
teacher/ukpage.htm

The Sports Page of The School Page UK carries good sets of links to all major and many minor sports. It's a resource worth knowing about, but it takes time to get it. The School Page UK has a lot of slow-loading graphics, and the Sports Page (a frame within it) has all the links on one page, making it a very large file.

When you have downloaded the Sports Page, save the file. (In Netscape use **Save Frame**.) Next time you want the links, open the file on your disk.

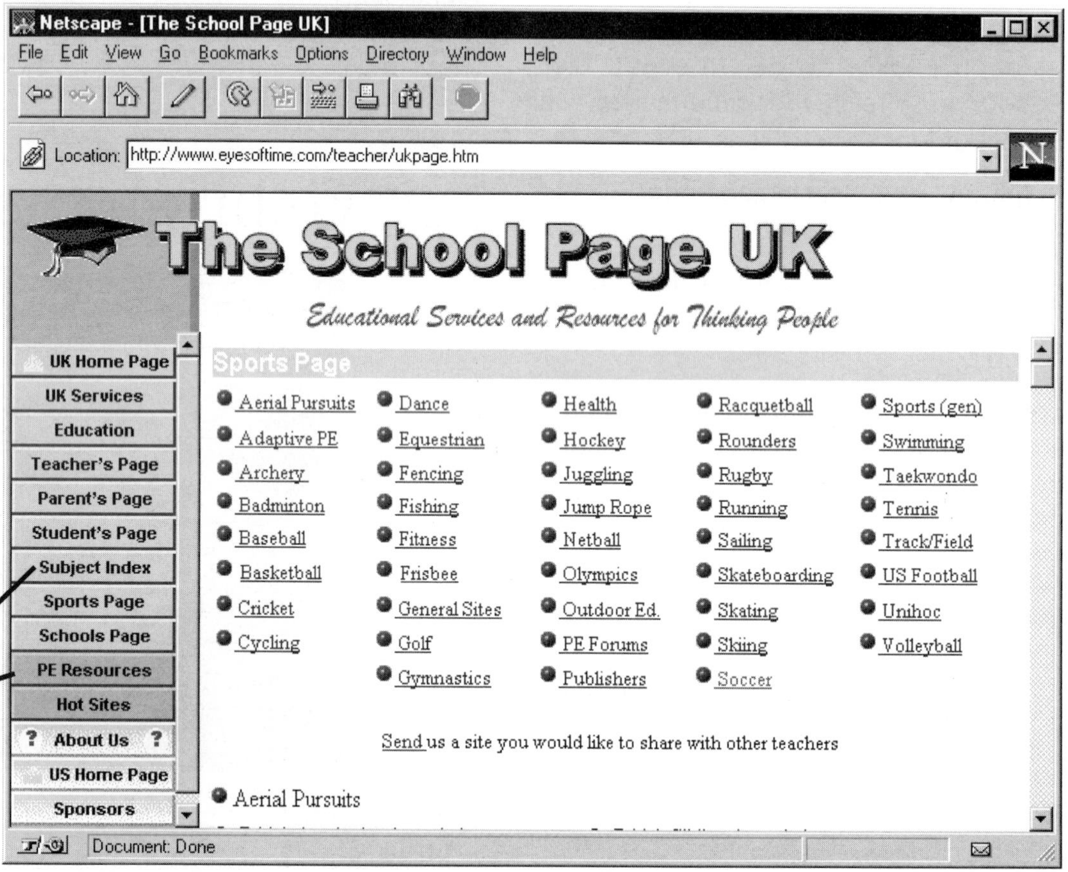

The other pages are
also worth visiting.

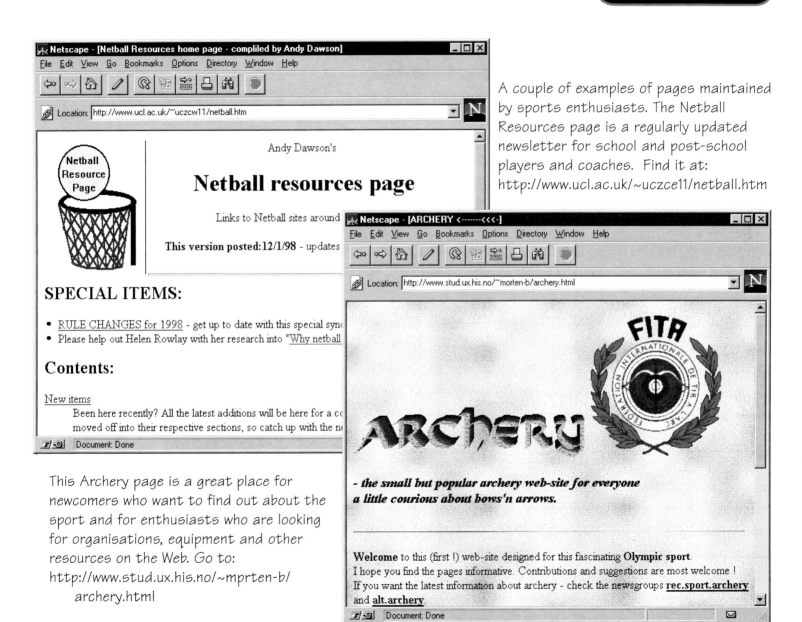

A couple of examples of pages maintained by sports enthusiasts. The Netball Resources page is a regularly updated newsletter for school and post-school players and coaches. Find it at: http://www.ucl.ac.uk/~uczce11/netball.htm

This Archery page is a great place for newcomers who want to find out about the sport and for enthusiasts who are looking for organisations, equipment and other resources on the Web. Go to: http://www.stud.ux.his.no/~mprten-b/ archery.html

Religious Education

If you want to know about different religions, there's plenty of first-hand information on the Internet – I don't think that there is a single faith which does not have at least one Web site run by its followers. Some of these give simple, factual introductions to their practices and beliefs; others have a more missionary flavour. It is obviously important to approach them all with an open mind, but in a spirit of critical enquiry.

Homework Heaven has a very comprehensive and well organised set of links on its **Religion** menu. This is an excellent place to start any general survey of other religions.

If you are looking for pages on any specific religion, you may be better off running a search at Infoseek or other search engine – though you may be swamped with links to some of the more popular and active religions.

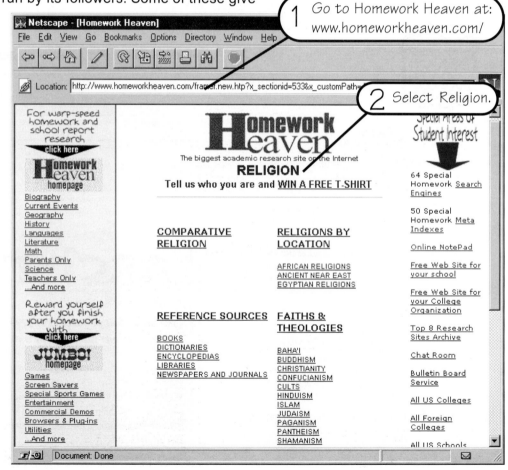

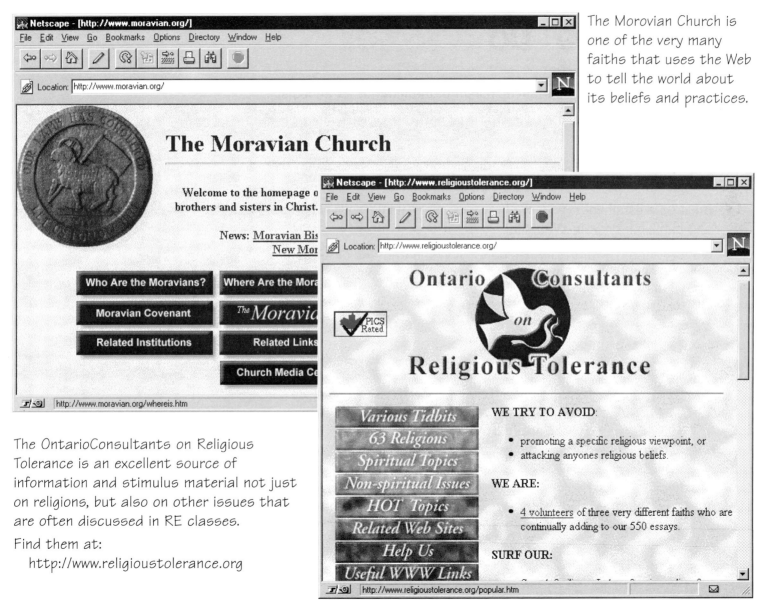

The Morovian Church is one of the very many faiths that uses the Web to tell the world about its beliefs and practices.

The OntarioConsultants on Religious Tolerance is an excellent source of information and stimulus material not just on religions, but also on other issues that are often discussed in RE classes.

Find them at:

http://www.religioustolerance.org

Things To Do

1 Make your contribution to the development of the Internet for schools!

◆ Take a small part of one of your subject areas and research it thoroughly.

◆ Start with the links, if any, at Yahoo and other directories, then use Infoseek and other search engines to track down relevant pages.

◆ Build up a list of links, with brief reviews, make it into an HTML page and publish it on your Web site.

◆ Go to Yahoo, UK directory, Heinemann World and any other central sites that invite contributions, and tell them about your page so that other people can find it.

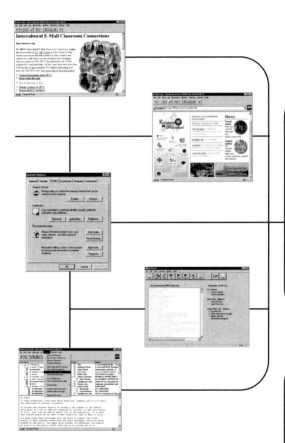

8 Stuff for staff

This chapter looks at some of the issues that schools should consider when starting to use the Internet. It does not aim to provide answers, but I hope it will help you to frame the questions that you should be raising with your local IT service and any potential access providers.

I have included a brief introduction to newsgroups here, as these are unlikely to be of much interest to pupils – at least in the early stages of their work on the Internet – though they can be useful sources for staff to explore.

Getting on-line

Equipment

You can, in theory, access the Internet using more or less any kind of computer, but the simple fact is that it is easier and cheaper to use a Window-based PC than anything else. At the time of writing, a bottom-of-the-range PC costs under £600, but is more than adequate for Internet work. Apple Macintoshes and Acorn Risc PCs will do a good job, but at around twice the price. Older Acorns will probably need upgrading – they must have at least 4 megabytes of RAM, for a start.

The only essential software is a Web browser. The two leaders, Netscape Navigator and Internet Explorer – both excellent – are available free for PCs and Apples. To get an equivalent browser for Acorns, you need to go to Ant and pay several hundred pounds for a site licence.

Of course, if your school has invested a lot of money in the development of an Acorn-based system, and there are enthusiasts on the staff who are willing to spend time collecting and installing the necessary software, then stick with Acorns. But if the choice is between a major upgrade, or the phased replacement of Acorns with PCs, then greater suitability of PC for Internet work is another factor to be taken into account.

Internet Access

To get onto the Internet you need a phone connection and an access provider.

The **phone connection** can be a fast ISDN line, where you pay a set fee no matter how much it is used, or a normal dial-up line, where you pay by the second. Dial-up lines make sense in small schools or when you are first testing the waters and only adding a few hours a week to the phone bill.

When choosing an **access provider,** there are three main considerations: child safety, reliability and cost.

The school must take all reasonable steps to ensure that its pupils are not exposed to the unsuitable material through the Internet. (See page 143 for more on this.)

The provider must have sufficient capacity to give you a reliable connection – the Internet suffers from 'traffic jams' at times, so the least you can do is make sure that you won't face bottlenecks at the first junction. (Though the first bottleneck could be your phone line – every line has a limit to how much data can be pushed through.)

Cost will depend largely on how many users are to have access at any time. Will you have a couple of machines in the library (around £200 a year), or half a dozen fully-wired classrooms (around £2,000 for a site licence).

As a first step, talk to your LEA's IT service. Some are able to act as access providers, and should be able to offer a child-safe, reliable and competitive service. If you already have a dedicated line to the LEA, for your financial management, it may be possible to use this for your Internet connection. Even if the LEA cannot offer access themselves, they should be able to give you informed advice about local providers.

RM's **Internet For Learning** (http://ifl-guide.rmplc.co.uk) and BT's **CampusWorld** (http://www.campus.bt.com) are both access and content providers. Subscribing to either of these services gives you access to their member-only educational sites as well as to the wider Internet – or just the safer parts of it.

Any commercial access provider should also be able to handle your connection – possibly at a lower cost – but is unlikely to have child-safety measures built into their system. The school would have to install its own protection software (see page 146).

Web e-mail

As its contribution to the UK NetYear project, Excite is offering free Web e-mail (see page 67) to all pupils and staff of UK schools. The offer is interesting, though neither as unique nor as altruistic as it may first appear. Many Net directories offer free Web e-mail to anyone –

to get your mail you have to visit their site and read their adverts, and advertising rates depend upon the number of visitors they get.

Web e-mail simplifies e-mail management within school. All pupils – in fact, everyone in the school – can have the same user name to get on-line, and old messages are stored in the on-line mailboxes, reducing the load on the disks in your machines.

On the other hand, Web e-mail is not convenient to use, as reading and writing is done on-line. Also, the school will find it difficult to monitor the pupils' use of e-mail.

Even where pupils have their own school-based e-mail addresses, the more enterprising ones could sign up for their own Web e-mail. If this is seen as a problem, the school will have to bar access to the e-mail sites.

Management and support

If a school is to make good use of the Internet, it must allow adequate teacher and support staff time.

Someone must be responsible for allocating user names and e-mail addresses to staff and pupils. Someone must install and maintain the browsers and other software – safety software will need special management. Someone must monitor disk usage – over-filled mailboxes and downloaded software can clog up a system.

If the school decides to build a Web site, someone must put it together – a considerable investment of time, and keep it up to date – a continuing time commitment.

Teachers must have time to familiarise themselves with the Internet as a whole and with the resources for their subject. An INSET day is a start, but it will not be enough.

Phased not fazed

Don't try to put everyone on-line at once – this is a recipe for confusion and worse. A phased startup is more likely to succeed. You do not have to put all the school's computers on-line at once (if ever), and even when a computer has been connected, only those people who have been allocated user names will have access to the Internet. Allow a term for each of the introductory phases.

1 A few computers are set up with Internet access – ideally in staff workrooms. A small group of teachers and technicians are given user names. While they are exploring the Internet, they should try out several browsers and other software and decide which to use. They should also test the reliability and safety of the connection through the access provider.

2 Enough computers are connected for all staff to have easy access, but only staff are given user names. Those teachers who will be involved at the next phase must get up to speed now. Other members of staff should at least start to explore the potential uses for their own subject areas.

3 One or two classes, or a group of volunteers, are brought on-line. Any potential problems over access, disk usage and security should appear at this stage. Can the phone line handle as many users as are likely to be on at any one time? Is there enough disk space in the network servers and in individual computers for mail messages and other downloaded files? Can pupils get to places they shouldn't? These questions must be resolved before moving to phase 4.

4 The rest of the school is brought on-line, perhaps in year groups, and possibly over two or three years.

Viruses

You cannot catch a virus browsing Web pages, but they may be hidden in downloaded program files (graphics and other data files are safe). Guard against infection with these precautions:

Install anti-virus software on all computers.

Only download from reputable software sites.

If you receive a file attached to e-mail, check it with your anti-virus software before running it.

Using the Web

Lesson preparation

It's very easy to waste time on the Internet – even when you are trying not to! Simply asking pupils to use the Web to find out something about, say, volcanoes, is likely to be unproductive. They will find thousands of sites, some of which may be relevant and at a suitable level; some will be fascinating but irrelevant; others will be too high or too low a level for the class.

Asking them to research a closely-defined topic, such as the eruption on Montserrat, is more likely to bring results, but the pupils must have good search skills to be able to carry this off. As a general rule, pupils should be sent to specific sites, to find specific information.

Track down the Internet resources yourself first. Visit the sites and decide which pages you want the pupils to read and what you want them to focus on.

You must provide a reliable way for pupils to reach those sites. Simply telling them the URLs won't work – once you get past the top page of any site, URLs tend to get complex. Bookmarks or clickable links are the answer.

If the class has access to only one computer, then it is simplest to use that computer for your own research, and to store the pages as Bookmarks. Ideally, you should organise the Bookmarks so that there is a separate sub-menu for each topic.

If pupils will be working on a number of computers, then the best solution is to write the links into an HTML page, and put that page up on your internal network or on your Web site. The links could be accompanied by notes and questions about the sites, to save producing a separate worksheet.

Technician support may be needed for those staff who do not have the skills or the time to create Web pages.

Pupil preparation

Before you start to send pupils off into the Internet, they need to know enough of the rudiments to be able to make good use of it. They must know how to:

◆ Get on-line.

◆ Navigate with links, Bookmarks and the Back button.

◆ Print pages.

◆ Copy text into a word-processor.

◆ Save images onto disk.

TeacherNet UK

This key site for teachers is at:
http://www.teachernetuk.org.uk

Classroom connections Pen pals

If you want to find other schools for joint projects or international e-mail exchanges, here are two places worth trying.

Intercultural E-mail Classroom Connections

IECC is based in the USA, but international in scope. Its Web site is simply for information – the real work is done through three mailing lists. These are sent out regularly to subscribers, and contain announcements from schools looking for partners to join in classroom projects, surveys or regular e-mail exchanges.

To subscribe to one of the lists, send an e-mail containing the single word 'subscribe' in the text of the message, to:

IECC-REQUEST@STOLAF.EDU   for the main IECC list

IECC-PROJECTS-REQUEST@STOLAF.EDU   for the projects list

IECC-SURVEYS-REQUEST@STOLAF.EDU   for the surveys list

You should start receiving the list in your e-mail within a few days.

If you want to know more about the IECC, go to **http://www.iecc.org**.

European Schoolnet

This is one of the main sites for European cooperation through the Web. Among other things, it has a Contact Gallery for schools that want to run joint projects. In general, there are fewer schools on-line elsewhere in Europe than in the UK – France has relatively few, which is a bit of a shame for those many UK schools that teach French is the first foreign language.

If you are looking for pen pals in other parts of Europe, try the Pen pals page at European Schoolnet.

For key pals elsewhere, try the Key Pals page in the students & pupils area at Heinemann World:

http://www.heinemann.co.uk

Or head for the Link Up page at Eduweb, and find yourself a Netpal:

http://www.eduweb.co.uk

Caution!

People are not always what they seem on the Internet.

Some people will hide their real age or pretend to be the opposite sex.

Be suspicious of anyone who asks for your real name and address or phone number on the first contact or after just a few e-mails.

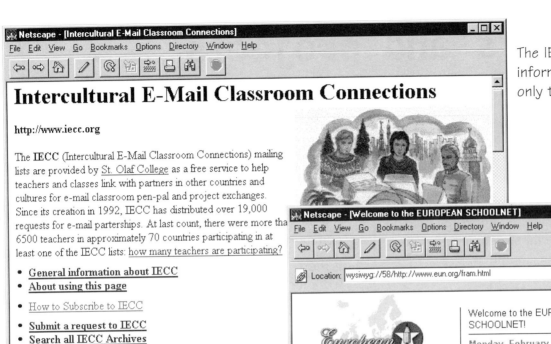

The IECC Web site is purely for information. Contacts are made only through its mailing lists.

There are many interesting projects and activities going on through European Schoolnet. The home page can be reached at:

http://www.eun.org

For one-to-one e-mail links, go to Penpal corner.

For classroom projects, head for the Contact Gallery.

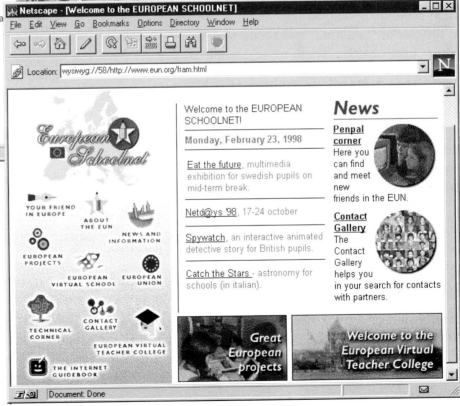

141

E-mail links and projects

A joint e-mail project with a class in another country can be valuable in many curriculum areas – Modern Languages, Geography and RE are the obvious ones, but joint science investigations, historical research, cross-cultural art and music are other possibilities.

As well as providing the enriched learning experiences, such projects should widen students' horizons, helping to break down national and racial stereotypes by direct contact with individuals in other countries.

Integration with other work

Clearly, the content should fit into your scheme of work (or into that of the linked school), but the timing should also be integrated. You can control when e-mails are sent, but do you know when incoming messages will arrive, so that they can be used in a lesson?

Practical implications

Do you need to review (and correct?) outgoing mail or preview incoming mail?

Should students work individually or in small groups?

Do you need to book time in an IT room to send and receive messages?

Tips for successful projects

◆ You must be familiar with sending and reading e-mail and have established good relationships with your distant colleagues before you involve students.

◆ Make sure that students know how to create and send e-mail – by writing to each other – before opening communications with your partner school.

◆ If there are not enough computers, plan alternative work for students who are not at the keyboard.

◆ Working in teams of two or three makes writing faster.

◆ Encourage students to keep their e-mail messages short, and to reply promptly to incoming mail.

◆ Students should keep a record of their interaction – and keep your own record of who is writing to whom, and of all the e-mail addresses.

UK NetYear

The government intends that this should become a focal point for the Internet in education. It had just opened at the time of writing, but should be worth a visit by now. See what's happening at:

http://www.uknetyear.org

Safe surfing

The Internet is a treasure trove of good things, but its darker corners contain much that should not be seen in schools. Pornography is one of the most common – and the most profitable – use of Web sites, and many news-groups (page 148) carry pornography, sexist, racist and other offensive material. Schools must take steps to ensure that none of this can be accessed by their pupils.

Access provider filtering

One of the simplest and most effective solutions is to get your access provider to do the filtering for you. RM's Internet For Learning and BT's CampusWorld both screen out unsuitable Web sites and newsgroups. Where LEAs offer access to the Internet through their networks, this would normally be filtered in the same way.

E-mail can also be automatically checked for the presence of certain words.

Safety software

An alternative is to install protection software on those computers that are used for Internet access. There are several approaches to protection.

◆ Some programs keep lists of *acceptable* sites and ban access to all others. This is the basis of Internet Explorer's Content Advisor(see page 144), amongst others. It is effective, but can be over-restrictive.

There are many acceptable sites and newsgroups which have not been checked and added to the lists.

◆ Some keep lists of *unacceptable* sites, and here the main problem is to keep the lists up to date as new sites are appearing all the time. Net Nanny (see page 146) and others that take this approach issue regular updates to their registered users.

◆ Incoming and outgoing text can be screened for key words. This keeps on eye on e-mail and newsgroup use, as well as Web sites, but can let unacceptable pictures slip through.

No filtering system is guaranteed 100% child-safe, as new Web sites and newsgroups are appearing all the time, and the unsuitable ones are not spotted and screened out immediately. If you leave the filtering to your service provider you at least have the assurance that someone is working on it – and that no-one in the school can tamper with it!

Rating systems

To find out more about these, go to the Recreational Standards Advisory Council – the rating organisation used by Internet Explorer (**http://www.rsac.org/**); or to SafeSurf (**http://www.safesurf.com/lifegard.htm**) another prominent rating organisation.

Safe Exploring

Internet Explorer 4.0 has a Content Advisor that can be activated to restrict the browser to sites rated by the (RSAC) Recreational Standards Advisory Council. At the time of writing over 50,000 sites have been rated, and these include most of the major resources of the Internet.

Sites are rated on their levels of sex, nudity, violence and bad language. On the Contents panel of the Internet Options, you can set the acceptable level for each aspect. If someone tries to go to a site with ratings beyond those limits – or that has not been rated – access is denied.

The settings are password-protected, and as the password can be used to override the restrictions – to visit an unrated but good site – it should be known by those members of staff who use the machine. This can raise problems in larger schools. If you have one password throughout the school, too many people are going to know it, and it is likely to leak out. If you have different passwords for each machine, the technicians will to have to carry lists around – which is not a secure practice.

Content Advisor simply controls access to Web sites. It does not restrict access to the newsgroups, or provide any supervision over e-mail.

Control of access through Content Advisor makes sense where there are few machines connected to the Internet, where your service provider offers a restricted set of newsgroups, and where pupils have no direct e-mail access.

1 Open the View menu and select Internet Options.

2 Go to the Content panel.

3 Click Enable...

Internet Options

General | Security | Content | Connection | Programs | Advanced

Content Advisor
Ratings help you control the Internet content that can be viewed on this computer.

Enable... | Settings...

Certificates
Use certificates to positively identify authorities and publishers.

Personal... | Authorities... | Publishers...

Personal information
Microsoft Profile Assistant stores your name, address, and other personal information.

Edit Profile...
Reset Sharing...

Microsoft Wallet provides a secure place to store private information for Internet shopping.

Addresses...
Payments...

OK | Cancel | Apply

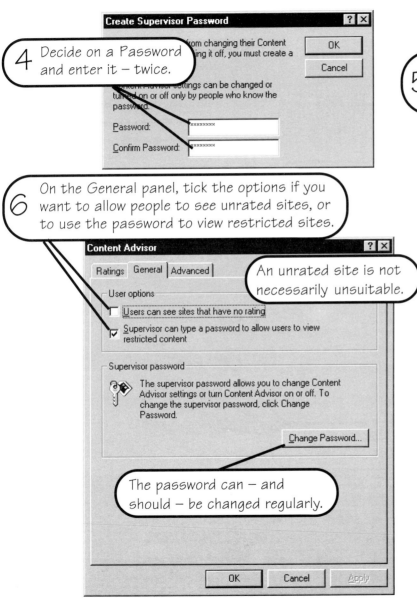

Create Supervisor Password [?][X]

4 Decide on a Password and enter it – twice.

...from changing their Content ...ing it off, you must create a

Content Advisor settings can be changed or turned on or off only by people who know the password.

Password: ××××××××
Confirm Password: ××××××××

OK
Cancel

6 On the General panel, tick the options if you want to allow people to see unrated sites, or to use the password to view restricted sites.

Content Advisor [?][X]

Ratings | General | Advanced

An unrated site is not necessarily unsuitable.

User options

☐ Users can see sites that have no rating

☑ Supervisor can type a password to allow users to view restricted content

Supervisor password

The supervisor password allows you to change Content Advisor settings or turn Content Advisor on or off. To change the supervisor password, click Change Password.

Change Password...

The password can – and should – be changed regularly.

OK   Cancel   Apply

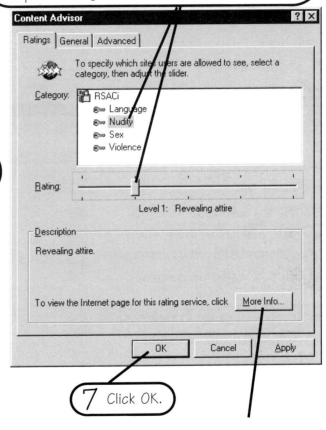

5 On the Ratings panel, set the limit for each Category – moving the slider to the right permits higher levels of sex'n'violence.

Content Advisor [?][X]

Ratings | General | Advanced

To specify which sites users are allowed to see, select a category, then adjust the slider.

Category:
🔒 RSACi
 🔵∞ Language
 🔵∞ Nudity
 🔵∞ Sex
 🔵∞ Violence

Rating: |——————[ ]——————|

Level 1:   Revealing attire

Description

Revealing attire.

To view the Internet page for this rating service, click More Info...

OK   Cancel   Apply

7 Click OK.

Click here while on-line to find out about the RSAC

Net Nanny

Net Nanny is one of the best protection programs. It stores lists of unacceptable words and unsuitable Web sites and newsgroups. When an attempt is made to access a site or group on the list, Net Nanny can respond in one or more ways:

◆ log the attempt, and leave you to take the appropriate action after you have checked the logs.

◆ issue a warning.

◆ block the move.

◆ shut down the program – that'll teach 'em!

Net Nanny lets you:

◆ set up your own lists of unacceptable words and places;

◆ allocate override permission to authorised users;

◆ it can also be set to supervise all Windows-based activity.

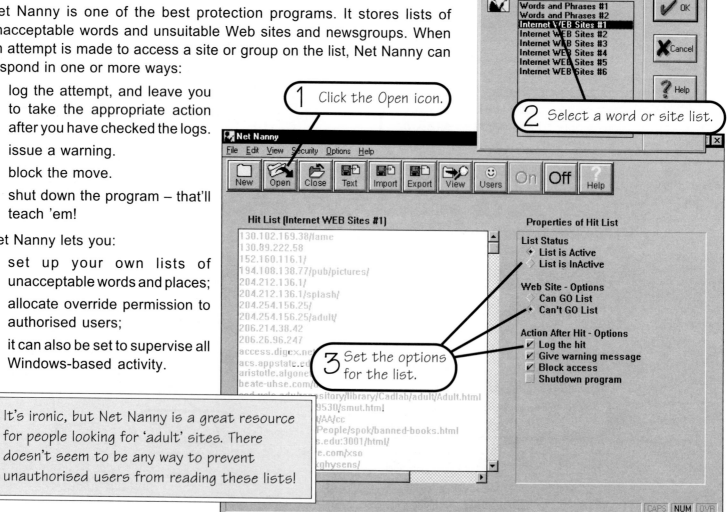

1 Click the Open icon.

2 Select a word or site list.

3 Set the options for the list.

It's ironic, but Net Nanny is a great resource for people looking for 'adult' sites. There doesn't seem to be any way to prevent unauthorised users from reading these lists!

The Log file

This records every significant action that occurs while Net Nanny is running. You will notice here that someone has been trying to get to the more exotic parts of the Internet!

The Log must be cleared regularly to keep it a manageable size. Anyone can do this, but the 'clear' operation is recorded!

◆ An unauthorised user can turn Net Nanny off – but it will be recorded in the log file.

Authorised users

If you want to let adults to browse unhindered, you can make them authorised users with the ability to override a shutdown or restart the program when Net Nanny swings into action.

To create a new user, open the User list, click New then enter the Name and Password and set the options.

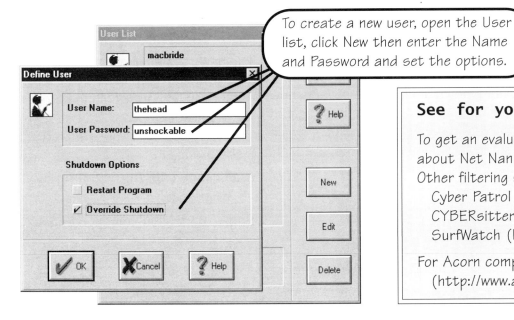

See for yourself

To get an evaluation copy or more information about Net Nanny, go to http://www.netnanny.com Other filtering software for the PC includes:
  Cyber Patrol (http://water.net/cpatrol.htm)
  CYBERsitter (http://www.solidoak.com/)
  SurfWatch (http://www.surfwatch.com/)

For Acorn computers, try Fresco, from Ant
  (http://www.ant.co.uk)

Newsgroups

Newsgroup names

Newsgroups are a kind of electronic cross between newsletters and noticeboards, where people can share information (and pictures and other files). There are over 25,000 groups, each dedicated to a different interest – professions and obsessions, programming languages and TV programs, software, hobbies, politics.

The quality and quantity of the communications vary enormously. Some newsgroups circulate large volumes of interesting and relevant information; others carry few articles – or few of any interest. Some groups are mainly for discussions, others are more like open help-lines, where people can ask for – and often get – solutions to problems. Some newsgroups are moderated, i.e. they have someone who checks all incoming articles before broadcasting them. This reduces the quantity of irrelevant and/or boring post.

Getting the news

Newsgroups cannot be accessed directly through the Web. They can only be reached through your service provider's news server. This collects new articles several times a day from distribution points around the Internet and holds them for its users. Not all news servers carry all newsgroups – which can be a good thing! The seedier and steamier side of the Internet is mainly in the newsgroups. You must ensure that these cannot be accessed through the school, and the simplest way to do this is to use a service provider that offers a filtered set of newsgroups. The alternative is to install Net Nanny, or similar software on all the computers.

If you are new to the Internet, there is a group specially for you. It's *news.announce.newusers*. And look out for *Emily Postnews' Etiquette for USENET News Postings*. It's posted fairly often.

Newsgroups are organised into a branching structure, with major sections sub-divided by topic. Their names reflect this structure; e.g, *uk.education.maths* is in the *uk* section, which amongst other things covers *education*, and has a group concerned with *maths*.

In Netscape 3.0, the hierarchy of groups is displayed in its News window (see opposite). It can be difficult to find groups on a topic unless you know where to look!

The news system in Communicator's and Internet Explorer both have routines to let you search the groups for a particular word. Looking for 'english', for example, turned up these groups:

    alt.usage.english
    can.english
    misc.education.language.english
    uw.enlish-usage

News from Netscape

In any browser, the News window looks very like the Mail window, and is used in much the same way. The top left pane shows the newsgroups; the top right holds the headers of the current articles in the selected group; the large lower pane will display the text of an article when it is selected.

When the window opens, the top left pane shows only those groups to which you have subscribed. If you are on-line at the time, the system downloads the headers for these groups.

If you want to dip into other groups, or see what's available so that you can subscribe to some, you must display all the newsgroups.

> 1 From the Options menu, select Show All Newsgroups.

> 2 Open folders to see the groups they contain.

> 3 Click on a group to download its headers.

> 4 Click on a header to read the article.

The first time you try to read the news, the system will download the list of groups from your access provider's news server – this takes time!

Index